THE Way OF A Pilgrim

THE Way OF A Pilgrim

COMPLETE TEXT
AND READER'S GUIDE

DENNIS J. BILLY

Liguori
LIGUORI, MISSOURI

For my Godchildren
Paul, Anna, and Marie

ℰ

Published by Liguori Publications
Liguori, Missouri
http://www.liguori.org

Library of Congress Cataloging-in-Publication Data

Billy, Dennis Joseph.
    The way of a pilgrim : complete text and reader's guide / Dennis J. Billy.—1st ed.
        p.   cm.
    Includes bibliographical references.
    ISBN 0-7648-0568-1 (pbk.)
    1. Otkrovennye rasskazy strannika dukhovnomu svoemu otëiu. 2. Jesus prayer.
3. Spiritual life—Orthodox Eastern Church. 4. Orthodox Eastern Church—
Doctrines. I. Title.

BX382.O853 B55 2000
248.4'819—dc21   99-054857

Printed in the United States of America
04 03 02 01 00   5 4 3 2 1
First Edition

Contents

Introduction

"What sort of spiritual teaching are you wanting to get?"
he asked me. "What is it puzzling you?"

FROM *THE WAY OF A PILGRIM*

ℋ

Have you ever heard of *The Way of a Pilgrim*?[1] This spiritual
classic from mid-nineteenth-century Russian Orthodoxy contains the autobiographical reflections of an anonymous Russian peasant as he seeks first to understand and then to put into
practice the meaning of the apostle Paul's words in 1 Thessalonians
5:17: "Pray without ceasing."

In four short narratives, this wandering *strannik*—as he would
have been known in his day—introduces the reader to the essentials
of the *hesychast* method of prayer, better known to its adherents the
world over as the Jesus Prayer and presented in much greater depth
in the classical anthology of Orthodox spiritual teaching known as
The Philokalia.[2] The great achievement of *The Way* is that it simpli-
fies the teaching of this latter work without compromising its meaning. Its simple literary style, focused summaries, and straightforward
method of instruction make it an excellent introduction to what is
arguably the greatest spiritual treasure of Eastern Christianity. For
this reason alone, it provides spiritual directors with a unique opportunity to offer their directees a firm footing in a venerable tradition of conversing with God, one that can be traced back to the age
of the Church Fathers—and beyond. It also provides them with an

alternative understanding of spiritual guidance that will complement and enhance whatever Western models they may employ.

COMPLEMENTARY WORKS

But why wait? Why not go straight to the real thing? Why bother with a short introductory work when one can go straight to *The Philokalia* itself? Such questions must be raised and answered at the outset, lest readers think that by studying *The Way* they are somehow being deprived of the deepest insights of the *hesychast* tradition.

Four responses come immediately to mind. First, for all its depth of spiritual insight, *The Philokalia* suffers the same fate as most other large spiritual anthologies. As a series of texts written between the fourth and fifteenth centuries and compiled in the eighteenth, it lacks the literary cohesion needed to make it accessible to a large-scale audience. Few of today's readers would have the time or the inclination to digest the dense and often difficult material scattered throughout the five volumes of the critical English edition. For this reason, a shorter and simpler work, which does justice to the scope and spirit of *The Philokalia*, can serve a real purpose.

Second, since the two works complement rather than oppose each other, one can easily be read in the light of the other—and vice versa. Like *The Way's* wandering Pilgrim, who carries a copy of *The Philokalia* with him wherever he goes, readers may wish (and should be encouraged) to delve into the original sources as soon as possible. In doing so, they will be able to follow the spiritual journey of the *strannik* with more insight and greater understanding.

Third, the narrative style of *The Way* invites readers not only to accompany the Pilgrim on his journey but also to enter into and identify with his spiritual experiences. There is a huge difference between combing through volumes of a number of highly concentrated and often enigmatic spiritual treatises (as one does when reading *The Philokalia*) and accompanying someone on a deeply intense and personal spiritual journey (as one does when reading *The Way*). The autobiographical character of the latter, moreover, encourages readers to reflect on the relevance of the Jesus Prayer for their own lives.

Fourth, and finally, over the last hundred years, *The Way of a Pilgrim* has become a spiritual classic in its own right—and has even inspired a sequel![3] It does for *The Philokalia* what *The Philokalia* does for the Bible, that is, provides the necessary lens that allows readers to gaze upon a dazzling and overwhelming light. As such, it speaks in a simple, unpretentious manner to people of all ages, classes, and cultural backgrounds.

METHOD

In addition to the above reasons, the whole question of method also comes into play. The narrative style of *The Way* lends itself to a particular approach of treating the theme of spiritual guidance in terms of a fourfold method of summary, reflection, query, and activity. The purpose of this method is to help readers chew, digest, circulate, and be nourished by the book's rich spiritual provisions. Just how is this done?

To begin with, each narrative is broken down into its basic parts and then summarized. The number of these parts will vary according to the length of the narratives themselves and how they are fit together internally. These summaries also serve the function of highlighting the main points of the story so that readers do not have to refer back constantly to the text of *The Way* itself.

The reflections that follow each section have a threefold purpose: (1) to highlight what each section teaches about prayer in general, (2) about the Jesus Prayer in particular, and (3) about the ministry of spiritual direction. These sections make explicit what is often only implicit in the teaching of *The Way* itself. Although they in no way claim to be an exhaustive treatment of the spiritual content of the book, they do highlight the major areas of concern and serve as helpful guides for future study. Particular emphasis is made in each of these reflection sections on the practical significance the teaching of *The Way* might have for the lives of ordinary believers.

After a brief concluding section at the end of each commentary, the purpose of which is to recall the spiritual thrust of each narrative and to find its place in the overall movement of the work, there follows two practical helps: (1) a series of reflection questions that encourage readers to examine the teaching of *The Way* in the concrete circumstances of their own lives, and (2) a series of exercises intended to help readers attain a more experiential knowledge of the matter at hand. In each of these sections, a special effort is also made to guide readers' reflections on the general state of their prayer life and on their understanding the ministry of spiritual direction. In the light of these more general reflection questions and activities, those that concern the Jesus Prayer and the nature of spiritual guidance in *The Way* can be more deeply appreciated and thus stand out in even greater relief.

The above method of summary, reflection, query, and activity is open-ended in both scope and purpose. It seeks not to impart an exhaustive knowledge of the spiritual teaching of *The Way* (and much less of *The Philokalia*), but only to help readers initiate a process of reflection. This process will ultimately help readers arrive at a deeper understanding of their own model of spiritual direction and to see what elements of the tradition of spiritual guidance present in *The Way* might be applicable to it. The thrust of this method is not to win adherents to a particular approach to spiritual guidance, but to invite readers to discover what elements of that tradition resonate within their own hearts and can be incorporated into their own spirituality. In doing so, it hopes to introduce readers to the most relevant spiritual insights into one of the great classics of Christian literature.

OBSERVATIONS

At this point, some further comments on the notion of spiritual guidance in *The Way of a Pilgrim* are in order. In these remarks, we will seek to draw the interpretative parameters within which a focused and highly sensitive reading of the work can occur. Through them, we will also try to inform readers of the limitations of the work when used as a tool in spiritual direction.

1. We remind readers that *The Way* was written in the cultural milieu of nineteenth-century Czarist Russia and includes many areas that simply do not translate in other historical contexts (for example, matters of diet, dress, means of transportation—to name but a few). For this reason, readers should be wary of any attempt to make a literal interpretation and application to the present day on every point. In reading *The Way*, the purpose should not be to imitate the life of the wandering Pilgrim in each and every detail, but to make appropriate judgments about the spiritual life that can be applied analogously to one's current situation.

2. That is not to say that there is nothing in the book that can be applied across a variety of historical and cultural contexts. On the contrary, the central teaching of the *hesychast* tradition claims that Jesus is the Lord of History and that the invocation of his holy name in the concrete circumstances of life will produce beneficial effects in both the internal and external lives of believers. Those effects show themselves in a gradual conversion that ultimately enables readers to see the hand of God in all the circumstances of life.

3. The book, moreover, is not a manual of prayer but the story of a particular man's search for God. As such, readers should refrain from referring to it for step-by-step directions on how to pray the

Jesus Prayer and thus realize the apostle's exhortation of constant prayer. While it is true that specific advice is offered from time to time on what must be done to achieve the state of unceasing prayer, this is always adapted to the circumstances of particular individuals and is especially suited to fit them at that particular moment of life. It would be a mistake, therefore, to offer such advice indiscriminately to each and every situation without regard for the situation of the individual in question. To do so would relegate prayer to the level of a system and overlook the fundamental relational understanding of prayer as a communion of hearts.

4. When going through the book, readers should also remember that the work was an important expression of lay spirituality for its day. The Pilgrim is a poor layman with little or no formal education. His determination to discover the secrets of constant prayer, however, leads him to the summit of the spiritual life and reminds readers that sanctity is meant not just for an elect few but for everyone. The Pilgrim addresses his autobiographical account to anyone who is willing to listen. It affirms the availability of God's grace to anyone who can say with sincerity of heart: "Lord Jesus Christ, have mercy on me!" This emphasis on the universal call to holiness was an important shift in the religious outlook of the Pilgrim's day and is now accepted by many as a fundamental principle of the spiritual life.

5. Part of the reason why the Pilgrim adopts such a simple lifestyle is so that he can identify with others on the basis of their common humanity. This enables him to help many people from all walks of society: nobles and serfs; priests and laity; men, women, and children; the weak and the strong. The Pilgrim, we might say, represents the attempt to strip ourselves of as many material, cultural, and intellectual superfluities as possible in order to get in touch with our own naked humanity. Only by doing so, can the Pilgrim uncover the common bond that he shares with all people and help them to recognize their weakness and frailty before God and one another.

6. Part of the great success and popularity of the book has to do with the way it presents the outward journey of the Pilgrim as a reflection of the interior journey of his heart. Throughout the account, readers follow the movement of the Jesus Prayer from the Pilgrim's body (as he recites it with his lips) to his mind (as he allows it to live in his thoughts) to his spirit (when it finally penetrates and touches his heart). As such, the Jesus Prayer allows the whole person to relate to God: body, mind, and spirit. It recognizes these important anthropological dimensions of human existence and offers individuals an integrated way of relating to God on each of them.

7. Two people play two different yet complementary roles in the life of the Pilgrim: his *starets,* who introduces him to and instructs him in the secrets of the Jesus Prayer (the first and second narratives), and his spiritual father, who listens to him as he narrates his earlier life experiences (the third and fourth narratives). These two functions of instruction and active listening enable the Pilgrim to deepen his spiritual life and to understand more clearly the meaning of his spiritual journey. They provide the parameters within which spiritual guidance takes place in the book and comes together in the Pilgrim's own approach of offering spiritual guidance to others (for example, when he listens to their stories and helps them to pray the Jesus Prayer).

8. Finally, throughout the book it is really the Spirit of God who leads the Pilgrim on his spiritual journey—no one else. All the external aids—the Bible, *The Philokalia*, the *starets*, even the Jesus Prayer itself—are nothing but instruments of the one divine purpose. It is through constant prayer that persons are able to commune with the Spirit of God in the depths of their soul. It is the Spirit who teaches the Pilgrim this interior prayer of the heart and who enables the Pilgrim to sense the activity of God's hand in the daily circumstances of his life. Without the Spirit, the Pilgrim's way would be nothing but purposeless wandering. With the Spirit, his way has meaning, direction, and constant peace.

CONCLUSION

The Way of a Pilgrim is a deeply spiritual but immensely practical work. Its ability to communicate the profound insights of *The Philokalia* in a simple, easy-to-understand, narrative style has enabled it to reach a wide audience and to spur interest in a deeper study of the writings from which it got its inspiration. As a text for spiritual guidance, it offers us hope that the apostle's exhortation "to pray without ceasing" can be realized in the concrete circumstances of life. It does this simply by lifting our hearts to God and saying, "Lord Jesus Christ, have mercy on me."

The words of the Jesus Prayer say all that ever really needs to be said. However they are prayed—on the lips, in the mind, in the heart—when prayed with sincerity, they are heard by God and responded to as only God can respond to them: with the gift of grace. The more they are prayed, the more God responds. The deeper they penetrate a person's heart, the more that person is permeated and led by the Spirit of God.

In this book, we hope to apply the richness of *The Way* and the *hesychast* tradition it represents to some of the pressing spiritual concerns of our day, especially those dealing with the ministry of spiritual direction. By focusing on a theme of spiritual guidance and by employing a practical method that asks concrete questions about the nature of one's spiritual journey, we hope to provide an opportunity for both directors and directees alike to examine the dynamics of their relationship and to determine if they are in any way impeding the movement of God's Spirit in their lives. With this in mind, we present the four narratives of *The Way of a Pilgrim*, each followed by a chapter of commentary and supplemental exercises. It is hoped that this narrative/commentary framework will help illuminate and diffuse the faith and spirit of the wandering Pilgrim to an ever wider audience in a practical and personal way.

Narrative I

The Way of a Pilgrim

✿

By the grace of God I am a Christian man, by my actions a great
sinner, and by calling a homeless wanderer of the humblest
birth who roams from place to place. My worldly goods are a
knapsack with some dried bread in it on my back, and in my breast
pocket a Bible. And that is all.

On the twenty-fourth Sunday after Pentecost I went to church
to say my prayers there during the liturgy. The First Epistle of Saint
Paul to the Thessalonians was being read, and among other words I
heard these: *"Pray without ceasing."* It was this text, more than any
other, which forced itself upon my mind, and I began to think how
it was possible to pray without ceasing, since a man has to concern
himself with other things also in order to make a living. I looked at
my Bible, and with my own eyes read the words which I had heard:
that we ought always, at all times and in all places, to pray with
uplifted hands. I thought and thought, but knew not what to make
of it. "What ought I to do?" I thought. "Where shall I find someone
to explain it to me? I will go to the churches where famous preachers are to be heard; perhaps there I shall hear something which will
throw light on it for me." I did so. I heard a number of very fine
sermons on prayer; what prayer is, how much we need it, and what
its fruits are; but no one said how one could succeed in prayer. I

heard a sermon on spiritual prayer and unceasing prayer, but how it was to be done was not pointed out.

Thus, listening to sermons failed to give me what I wanted and, having had my fill of them without gaining understanding, I gave up going to hear public sermons. I settled on another plan—by God's help to look for some experienced and skilled person who would teach me about unceasing prayer which drew me so urgently.

For a long time I wandered through many places. I read my Bible always, and everywhere I asked whether there was not in the neighborhood a spiritual teacher, a devout and experienced guide, to be found. One day I was told that in a certain village a gentleman had long been living and seeking the salvation of his soul. He had a chapel in his house. He never left his estate, and he spent his time in prayer and reading devotional books. Hearing this, I ran rather than walked to the village named. I got there and found him.

"What do you want of me?" he asked.

"I have heard that you are a devout and clever person," said I. "In God's name please explain to me the meaning of the apostle's words, *'Pray without ceasing.'* How is it possible to pray without ceasing? I want to know so much, but I cannot understand it at all."

He was silent for a while and looked at me closely. Then he said, "Ceaseless interior prayer is a continual yearning of the human spirit toward God. To succeed in this consoling exercise we must pray more often to God to teach us to pray without ceasing. Pray more, and pray more fervently. It is prayer itself which will reveal to you how it can be achieved unceasingly; but it will take some time."

So saying, he had food brought to me, gave me money for my journey, and let me go.

He did not explain the matter.

Again I set off. I thought and thought, I read and read. I dwelt over and over again upon what this man had said to me, but I could not get to the bottom of it. Yet so greatly did I wish to understand that I could not sleep at night.

I walked at least a hundred and twenty-five miles, and then I came to a large town, a provincial capital, where I saw a monastery. At the inn where I stopped I heard it said that the abbot was a man of great kindness, devout and hospitable. I went to see him. He met me in a very friendly manner, asked me to sit down, and offered me refreshment.

"I do not need refreshment, holy Father," I said, "but I beg you to give me some spiritual teaching. How can I save my soul?"

"What? Save your soul? Well, live according to the commandments, say your prayers, and you will be saved."

"But I hear it said that we should pray without ceasing, and I don't know how to pray without ceasing. I cannot even understand what unceasing prayer means. I beg you, Father, explain this to me."

"I don't know how to explain further, dear Brother. But, stop a moment. I have a little book, and it is explained there." And he handed me Saint Dmitri's book on *The Spiritual Education of the Inner Man*, saying, "Look, read this page."

I began to read as follows: "The words of the apostle, '*Pray without ceasing*,' should be understood as referring to the creative prayer of the understanding. The understanding can always be reaching out toward God, and pray to him unceasingly."

"But," I asked, "what is the method by which the understanding can always be turned toward God, never be disturbed, and pray without ceasing?"

"It is very difficult, even for one to whom God himself gives such a gift," replied the abbot.

He did not give me the explanation.

I spent the night at his house, and in the morning, thanking him for his kindly hospitality, I went on my way; where to, I did not know myself. My failure to understand made me sad and, by way of comforting myself, I read my Bible. In this way I followed the main road for five days.

At last toward evening I was overtaken by an old man who looked like a cleric of some sort. In answer to my question, he told

me that he was a monk belonging to a monastery some six miles off
the main road. He asked me to go there with him. "We take in pilgrims," said he, "and give them rest and food with devout persons
in the guest house." I did not feel like going. So in reply I said that
my peace of mind in no way depended upon my finding a resting
place, but upon finding spiritual teaching. Neither was I running
after food, for I had plenty of dried bread in my knapsack.

"What sort of spiritual teaching are you wanting to get?" he
asked me. "What is it puzzling you? Come now! Do come to our
house, dear Brother. We have *startsi*[4] of ripe experience well able to
give guidance to your soul and to set it upon the true path, in the
light of the word of God and the writings of the holy Fathers."

"Well, it's like this, Father," said I. "About a year ago, while I
was at the liturgy, I heard a passage from the epistles which bade
men pray without ceasing. Failing to understand, I began to read
my Bible, and there also in many places I found the divine command that we ought to pray at all times, in all places—not only
while about our business, not only while awake, but even during
sleep—*'sleep, but my heart is awake.'* This surprised me very much,
and I was at a loss to understand how it could be carried out and in
what way it was to be done. A burning desire and thirst for knowledge awoke in me. Day and night the matter was never out of my
mind. So I began to go to churches and to listen to sermons. But
however many I heard, from not one of them did I get any teaching
about how to pray without ceasing. They always talked about getting ready for prayer, or about its fruits and the like, without teaching one *how* to pray without ceasing, or what such prayer means. I
have often read the Bible and there made sure of what I have heard.
But meanwhile, I have not reached the understanding that I long
for, and so to this hour I am still uneasy and in doubt."

Then the old man crossed himself and spoke. "Thank God, my
dear Brother, for having revealed to you this unappeasable desire
for unceasing interior prayer. Recognize in it the call of God, and
calm yourself. Rest assured that what has hitherto been accomplished

in you is the testing of the harmony of your own will with the voice of God. It has been granted to you to understand that the heavenly light of unceasing interior prayer is attained neither by the wisdom of this world nor by the mere outward desire for knowledge, but that on the contrary, it is found in poverty of spirit and in active experience in simplicity of heart. That is why it is not surprising that you have been unable to hear anything about the essential work of prayer, and to acquire the knowledge by which ceaseless activity in it is attained.

"Doubtless a great deal has been preached about prayer, and there is much about it in the teaching of various writers. But since, for the most part, all their reasonings are based upon speculation and the working of natural wisdom, and not upon active experience, they sermonize about the qualities of prayer rather than about the nature of the thing itself. One argues beautifully about the necessity of prayer, another about its power and the blessings which attend it, a third again about the things which lead to perfection in prayer, that is, about the absolute necessity of zeal, an attentive mind, warmth of heart, purity of thought, reconciliation with one's enemies, humility, contrition, and so on. But what is prayer? And how does one learn to pray? Upon these questions, primary and essential as they are, one very rarely gets any precise enlightenment from present-day preachers. For these questions are more difficult to understand than all their arguments that I have just spoken of, and require mystical knowledge, not simply the learning of the schools. And the most deplorable thing of all is that the vain wisdom of the world compels them to apply the human standard to the divine.

"Many people reason quite the wrong way round about prayer, thinking that good actions and all sorts of preliminary measures render us capable of prayer. But quite the reverse is the case; it is prayer which bears fruit in good works and all the virtues. Those who reason so take, incorrectly, the fruits and the results of prayer for the means of attaining it, and this is to depreciate the power of prayer. And it is quite contrary to holy Scripture, for the apostle

Paul says, *'I exhort therefore that first of all supplications be made'* (1 Tim 2:1). The first thing laid down in the apostle's words about prayer is that the work of prayer comes before everything else: *'I exhort therefore that first of all....'* The Christian is bound to perform many good works but, before all else, what he ought to do is to pray, for without prayer no other good work whatever can be accomplished. Without prayer he cannot find the way to the Lord; he cannot understand the truth; he cannot crucify the flesh with its passions and lusts; his heart cannot be enlightened with the light of Christ; he cannot be savingly united to God. None of those things can be effected unless they are preceded by constant prayer. I say 'constant,' for the perfection of prayer does not lie within our power; as the apostle Paul says, *'For we know not what we should pray for as we ought'* (Rom 8:26). Consequently, it is just to pray often, to pray always, which falls within our power as the means of attaining purity of prayer, which is the mother of all spiritual blessings. 'Capture the mother and she will bring you the children,' said Saint Isaac the Syrian. Learn first to acquire the power of prayer and you will easily practice all the other virtues. But those who know little of this from practical experience and the profoundest teaching of the holy Fathers have no clear knowledge of it and speak of it but little."

During this talk, we had almost reached the monastery. And so as not to lose touch with this wise old man, and to get what I wanted more quickly, I hastened to say, "Be so kind, reverend Father, as to show me what prayer without ceasing means and how it is learnt. I see you know all about these things."

He took my request kindly and asked me into his cell. "Come in," said he. "I will give you a volume of the holy Fathers from which, with God's help, you can learn about prayer clearly and in detail."

We went into his cell and he began to speak as follows: "The continuous interior Prayer of Jesus is a constant uninterrupted calling upon the divine name of Jesus with the lips, in the spirit, in the heart, while forming a mental picture of his constant presence and imploring his grace during every occupation, at all times, in all places, even during sleep. The appeal is couched in these terms, 'Lord Jesus Christ, have mercy on me.' One who accustoms himself to this appeal experiences as a result so deep a consolation and so great a need to offer the Prayer always that he can no longer live without it, and it will continue to voice itself within him of its own accord. Now do you understand what prayer without ceasing is?"

"Yes indeed, Father, and in God's name teach me how to gain the habit of it," I cried, filled with joy. "Read this book," he said. "It is called *The Philokalia*[5] and it contains the full and detailed science of constant interior prayer set forth by twenty-five holy Fathers. The book is marked by a lofty wisdom and is so profitable to use that it is considered the foremost and best manual of the contemplative spiritual life. As the revered Nicephorus said, 'It leads one to salvation without labor and sweat.'"

"Is it then more sublime and holy than the Bible?" I asked.

"No, it is not that. But it contains clear explanations of what the Bible holds in secret and which cannot be easily grasped by our shortsighted understanding. I will give you an illustration. The sun is the greatest, the most resplendent, and the most wonderful of heavenly luminaries, but you cannot contemplate and examine it simply with unprotected eyes. You have to use a piece of artificial glass which is many millions of times smaller and darker than the sun. But through this little piece of glass you can examine the magnificent monarch of stars, delight in it, and endure its fiery rays. Holy Scripture also is a dazzling sun, and this book, *The Philokalia,* is the piece of glass which we use to enable us to contemplate the sun in its imperial splendor. Listen now, I am going to read you the sort of instruction it gives on unceasing interior prayer."

He opened the book, found the instruction by Saint Simeon the New Theologian, and read: "'Sit down alone and in silence. Lower your head, shut your eyes, breathe out gently, and imagine yourself looking into your own heart. Carry your mind, that is, your thoughts, from your head to your heart. As you breathe out say, "Lord Jesus

Christ, have mercy on me." Say it moving your lips gently, or simply say it in your mind. Try to put all other thoughts aside. Be calm, be patient, and repeat the process very frequently.'"

The old man explained all this to me and illustrated its meaning. We went on reading from *The Philokalia* passages of Saint Gregory of Sinai, Saint Callistus, and Saint Ignatius, and what we read from the book the *starets* explained in his own words. I listened closely and with great delight, fixed it in my memory and tried, as far as possible, to remember every detail. In this way we spent the whole night together and went to matins without having slept at all.

The *starets* sent me away with his blessing and told me that while learning the Prayer, I must always come back to him and tell him everything, making a very frank confession and report; for the inward process could not go on properly and successfully without the guidance of a teacher.

In church I felt a glowing eagerness to take all the pains I could to learn unceasing interior prayer, and I prayed to God to come to my help. Then I began to wonder how I should manage to see my *starets* again for counsel or confession, since leave was not given to remain for more than three days in the monastery guest house, and there were no houses near.

However, I learned that there was a village between two and three miles from the monastery. I went there to look for a place to live and, to my great happiness, God showed me the thing I needed. A peasant hired me for the whole summer to look after his kitchen garden and, what is more, gave me the use of a little thatched hut in it where I could live alone. God be praised! I had found a quiet place. And in this manner I took up my abode and began to learn interior prayer in the way I had been shown, and to go to see my *starets* from time to time.

For a week, alone in my garden, I steadily set myself to learn to pray without ceasing exactly as the *starets* had explained. At first, things seemed to go very well. But then it tired me very much. I felt lazy and bored and overwhelmingly sleepy, and a cloud of all sorts of other thoughts closed round me. I went in distress to my *starets* and told him the state I was in.

He greeted me in a friendly way and said, "My dear Brother, it is the attack of the world of darkness upon you. To that world, nothing is worse than heartfelt prayer on our part. And it is trying by every means to hinder you and to turn you aside from learning the Prayer. But all the same, the enemy only does what God sees fit to allow, and no more than is necessary for us. It would appear that you need a further testing of your humility, and that it is too soon, therefore, for your unmeasured zeal to approach the loftiest entrance to the heart. You might fall into spiritual covetousness. I will read you a little instruction from *The Philokalia* upon such cases."

He turned to the teaching of Nicephorus and read, "'If after a few attempts you do not succeed in reaching the realm of your heart in the way you have been taught, do what I am about to say, and by God's help you will find what you seek. The faculty of pronouncing words lies in the throat. Reject all other thoughts (you can do this if you will) and allow that faculty to repeat only the following words constantly, "Lord Jesus Christ, have mercy on me." Compel yourself to do it always. If you succeed for a time, then without a doubt your heart also will open to prayer. We know it from experience.'

"There you have the teaching of the holy Fathers on such cases," said my *starets,* "and therefore, you ought from today onwards to carry out my directions with confidence and repeat the Prayer of Jesus as often as possible. Here is a rosary (prayer cord). Take it and, to start with, say the Prayer three thousand times a day. Whether you are standing or sitting, walking or lying down, continually repeat 'Lord Jesus Christ, have mercy on me.' Say it quietly and without hurry, but without fail exactly three thousand times a day without deliberately increasing or diminishing the number. God will help you and by this means you will reach also the unceasing activity of the heart."

I gladly accepted this guidance and went home and began to

carry out faithfully and exactly what my *starets* had bidden. For two days I found it rather difficult, but after that it became so easy and likable that, as soon as I stopped, I felt a sort of need to go on saying the Prayer of Jesus, and I did it freely and willingly, not forcing myself to it as before.

I reported to my *starets,* and he bade me say the Prayer six thousand times a day, saying, "Be calm, just try as faithfully as possible to carry out the set number of prayers. God will vouchsafe you his grace."

In my lonely hut I said the Prayer of Jesus six thousand times a day for a whole week. I felt no anxiety. Taking no notice of any other thoughts, however much they assailed me, I had but one object, that is, to carry out my *starets'* bidding exactly. And what happened? I grew so used to my Prayer that when I stopped for a single moment I felt, so to speak, as though something were missing, as though I had lost something. The very moment I started the Prayer again, it went on easily and joyously. If I met anyone, I had no wish to talk to him. All I wanted was to be alone and to say my Prayer, so used to it had I become in a week.

My *starets* had not seen me for ten days. On the eleventh day he came to see me himself, and I told him how things were going. He listened and said, "Now you have got used to the Prayer. See that you preserve the habit and strengthen it. Waste no time, therefore, but make up your mind by God's help from today to say the Prayer of Jesus twelve thousand times a day. Remain in your solitude, get up early, go to bed late, and come and ask advice of me every fortnight."

I did as he bade me. The first day I scarcely succeeded in finishing my task of saying twelve thousand prayers by late evening. The second day I did it easily and contentedly. To begin with, this ceaseless saying of the Prayer brought a certain amount of weariness: my tongue felt numbed; I had a stiff sort of feeling in my jaws; I had a feeling—at first pleasant but afterwards slightly painful—in the roof of my mouth. The thumb of my left hand, with which I counted my beads, hurt a little. I felt a slight inflammation in the whole of that wrist and even up to the elbow, which was not unpleasant. Moreover, all this aroused me, as it were, and urged me on to frequent saying of the Prayer. For five days I did my set number of twelve thousand prayers and, as I formed the habit, I found at the same time pleasure and satisfaction in it.

Early one morning the Prayer woke me up as it were. I started to say my usual morning prayers, but my tongue refused to say them easily or exactly. My whole desire was fixed upon one thing only—to say the Prayer of Jesus and, as soon as I went on with it, I was filled with joy and relief. It was as though my lips and my tongue pronounced the words entirely of themselves without any urging from me. I spent the whole day in a state of the greatest contentment. I felt as though I was cut off from everything else. I lived as though in another world, and I easily finished my twelve thousand prayers by the early evening. I felt very much like still going on with them, but I did not dare to go beyond the number my *starets* had set me. Every day following I went on in the same way with my calling on the name of Jesus Christ, and that with great readiness and liking. Then I went to see my *starets* and told him everything frankly and in detail.

He heard me out and then said, "Be thankful to God that this desire for Prayer and this facility in it have been manifested in you. It is a natural consequence which follows constant effort and spiritual achievement. It can be compared to a machine whose wheel has been given a push, and which works for a while afterwards by itself; but if it is to go on working still longer, one must oil it and give it another push. Now you see with what admirable gifts God in his love for mankind has endowed even the bodily nature of man. You see what feelings can be produced even outside a state of grace in a soul which is sinful and with passions unsubdued, as you yourself have experienced. But how wonderful, how delightful, and how consoling a thing it is when God is pleased to grant the gift of self-acting spiritual prayer, and to cleanse the soul from all sensuality! It is a condition which is impossible to describe, and the discovery of this mystery of prayer is a foretaste on earth of the bliss of heaven. Such happiness is reserved for those who seek after God in the simplicity of a loving heart. Now I give you my permission to say your Prayer as often as you wish and as often as you can. Try to devote every moment you are awake to the Prayer, call on the name of Jesus Christ without counting the number of times, and submit yourself humbly to the will of God, looking to him for help. I am sure he will not forsake you, and that he will lead you into the right path."

Under this guidance I spent the whole summer in ceaseless oral prayer to Jesus Christ, and I felt absolute peace in my soul. During sleep I often dreamed that I was saying the Prayer. And during the day, if I happened to meet anyone, all men without exception were as dear to me as if they had been my nearest relations. But I did not concern myself with them much. All my ideas were quite calmed of their own accord. I thought of nothing whatever but my Prayer, my mind tended to listen to it, and my heart began of itself to feel at times a certain warmth and pleasure. If I happened to go to church, the lengthy service of the monastery seemed short to me and no longer wearied me as it had in time past. My lonely hut seemed like a splendid palace, and I knew not how to thank God for having sent to me, a lost sinner, so wholesome a guide and master.

But I was not long to enjoy the teaching of my dear *starets,* who was so full of divine wisdom. He died at the end of the summer. Weeping freely, I bade him farewell and thanked him for the fatherly teaching he had given my wretched self and, as a blessing and a keepsake, I begged for the rosary with which he said his prayers.

And so I was left alone. Summer came to an end and the kitchen garden was cleared. I had no longer anywhere to live. My peasant sent me away, giving me by way of wages two roubles, and filling up my bag with dried bread for my journey. Again I started off on my wanderings. But now I did not walk along as before, filled with care. The calling upon the name of Jesus Christ gladdened my way. Everybody was kind to me; it was as though everyone loved me.

Then it occurred to me to wonder what I was to do with the money I had earned by my care of the kitchen garden. What good was it to me? I no longer had a *starets,* there was no one to go on teaching me. Why not buy *The Philokalia* and continue to learn from it more about interior prayer?

I crossed myself and set off with my Prayer. I came to a large town, where I asked for the book in all the shops. In the end I found it, but they asked me three roubles for it, and I had only two. I bargained for a long time, but the shopkeeper would not budge an inch. Finally he said, "Go to this church nearby and speak to the church warden. He has a book like that, but it's a very old copy. Perhaps he will let you have it for two roubles." I went, and sure enough I found and bought for my two roubles a worn and old copy of *The Philokalia.* I was delighted with it. I mended my book as much as I could. I made a cover for it with a piece of cloth and put it into my breast pocket with my Bible.

And that is how I go about now, and ceaselessly repeat the Prayer of Jesus, which is more precious and sweet to me than anything in the world. At times I do as much as forty-three or forty-four miles a day, and do not feel that I am walking at all; I am aware only of the fact that I am saying my Prayer. When the bitter cold pierces me, I begin to say my Prayer more earnestly and I quickly get warm all over. When hunger begins to overcome me, I call more often on the name of Jesus and I forget my wish for food. When I fall ill and get rheumatism in my back and legs, I fix my thoughts on the Prayer and do not notice the pain. If anyone harms me, I have only to think, "How sweet is the Prayer of Jesus!" and the injury and the anger alike pass away and I forget it all.

I have become a sort of half-conscious person. I have no cares and no interests. The fussy business of the world I would not give a glance to. The one thing I wish for is to be alone and all by myself to pray, to pray without ceasing; and doing this, I am filled with joy. God knows what is happening to me! Of course, all this is sensuous or, as my departed *starets* said, an artificial state which follows naturally upon routine. But because of my unworthiness and stupidity, I dare not venture yet to go on further and learn and make my own spiritual prayer within the depths of my heart. I await God's time. And in the meanwhile, I rest my hope on the prayers of my departed *starets*. Thus, although I have not yet reached that ceaseless spiritual prayer which is self-acting in the heart, yet I thank God I do now understand the meaning of those words I heard in the epistle— *"Pray without ceasing."*

Commentary I
Journey of the Spirit

"What ought I to do?" I thought. "Where shall I find someone to explain it to me?"

FROM *THE WAY OF A PILGRIM*

৯৯

As the tale opens, we find the Pilgrim remembering the beginning of his spiritual quest and the circumstances surrounding it. These memories include his honest estimation of himself in the eyes of God and his fellow human beings, the specific origins of his spiritual query, his early attempts to satisfy it, and the relationship with his *starets*—his spiritual father or elder. Each of these memories plays a significant role in his—and our—ongoing search for understanding, and sheds important light on the nature of the spiritual-direction relationship.

THE PILGRIM'S SELF-ESTIMATION

Summary

At the outset of his autobiographical account, the anonymous author provides us with a succinct description of himself with respect to: God, his own freedom of choice, his vocation, and his possessions: (1) God's grace has made him a Christian; (2) his own actions, a sinner; (3) his vocation, a homeless wanderer of humble origins who possesses (4) nothing but a knapsack containing some bread and the Bible in his breast pocket.

Grace. Free will. Calling. Poverty. These four concepts provide the backdrop of the Pilgrim's own self-understanding. He is conscious of the presence of God's grace in his life and of his own tendency to rebel against it; he understands his pilgrim life in terms of a call, and recognizes his austerity of life as a necessary element of it.

Each of these elements also colors the Pilgrim's stance toward the world. As a Christian, he professes his belief in the fundamental goodness of creation and in the redemptive process wrought by Christ. As a sinner, he shares the plight of broken humanity and its need for forgiveness. As a homeless wanderer, he symbolizes—in the concrete circumstances of his life—the spiritual journey each person begins at the first moment of life. As a poor man, he reminds us of our own inner poverty and highlights for us the importance of both bodily *and* spiritual nourishment in our quest for wholeness. These "bare essentials" resonate in our hearts and strengthen our bond with the anonymous author. As a result, we can identify more closely with the exploits of this unknown spiritual wayfarer as he slowly makes his way across the back roads of nineteenth-century Czarist Russia.

Reflection

It bears noting that the author, who writes this brief self-description (a single paragraph of three sentences) in the present tense, quickly moves to the past tense when he begins recounting the details of his life's experiences. In doing so, he highlights the importance of recollection for the spiritual journey, a process that is selective by its very nature (it would be impossible for him to recall every detail), and that brings to the fore the necessity for us to do the same in our own tale of spiritual discovery (no one else will do it). In this way, the memories of this wandering Pilgrim remind us that God's hand in our lives is often manifested in hindsight, when we have had the time and the inclination to weave together a life-sized tapestry of our own salvation history using the multicolored threads of personal experience. The reflective tone of the Pilgrim's narrative thus challenges us to go back over our own lives to try to discover how God has led us in the past.

As far as spiritual guidance is concerned, the author stands within and writes for those who embrace the Christian tradition. Although he does so specifically as a member of Eastern Orthodoxy, his teaching is broad-based and universal enough for use by Latin Catholics and members of other Christian denominations. All those who acknowledge the abundance of God's grace accessible through the death and Resurrection of Jesus Christ and the invocation of his holy name can benefit from the teaching promulgated by this anonymous nineteenth-century wayfarer. The power of Jesus' name to transform the lives of believers dominates his reflections from beginning to end. The significance of this insight gives the author (and, through him, us) a deeper insight into the passing nature of sin's hold over the human heart. Although he is keenly aware of his own sinfulness, the author is even more aware of the power of God's grace to transform. He sees that the drama of the believer's pilgrimage through life involves the slow, steady process in which the power of Jesus' name permeates the life of the believer and finally defeats the powers of darkness at work in the human soul. In this respect, a person's entire life can be looked upon in terms of a spiritual journey. With bread in his knapsack and a Bible over his heart, the Pilgrim sets out—with us—in search of God and the way to salvation.

ORIGINS OF THE PILGRIM'S SPIRITUAL QUEST

Summary

After this brief introduction, the author lets us in on the circumstances that first gave rise to his life as a wandering pilgrim. He goes to church on the twenty-fourth Sunday after Pentecost and, while at worship, is struck by the words of the apostle Paul telling the Thessalonians "to pray without ceasing."[6] This one verse from Scripture becomes fixed in his mind, and he begins to wonder how a person could possibly perform such a feat. Must not he, at some point, be occupied with other matters? This one moment, a peak experience of his life, sets the tone for all that follows. The author is determined to discover what the apostle intends by this phrase. His life of wandering becomes a search for understanding the meaning of these mysterious words and putting them into effect. All else becomes secondary.

Reflection

A deeper understanding of this key formative experience in the author's life may shed light on the nature of his spiritual quest. To begin with, his account later suggests that he has been reared in the Christian faith and is accustomed to worshiping the divine liturgy on a regular basis. Based on such evidence, we can well assume that this is not the first time the Pilgrim has heard the apostle's startling words to the Thessalonians, but only the first time he has been struck by them and has determined to learn more about them. On this particular Sunday, the author is caught up in a moment of grace, a veritable confrontation with the divine. He finds himself in church (a holy place) on a Sunday (a holy time) worshiping God (a holy action) in the sacred liturgy (a holy sacrifice), and moved by the words of the epistle (in a holy listening). All of these have already become a routine part of his life and now come together in such a way that they shake up his world and give new purpose to his life. The words of the apostle affect both his mind and his heart. They become fixed in the former and lead the latter to wonder about the practical impact they would have on people's lives. This grace-filled interplay between mind and heart moves the Pilgrim to action and provides the poignant spiritual context for what lies ahead.

As far as spiritual direction is concerned, we should not expect the Pilgrim's story to be applicable in every detail. Because this is the Pilgrim's own personal account of the movement of God's grace in his life, it would be unrealistic of us to demand relevance in every respect. Be that as it may, we still should be encouraged to identify those moments of grace that have shaped the contours of our own spiritual journey. What were the peak moments—the holy times, places, actions, words, and questions—that have challenged our mind and moved our heart? By identifying such times and key events, we can make sense out of the spiritual journey they have given rise to and possibly even gain some insight into our own personal destiny. The end of our spiritual journey is hidden in the mystery of its origins. Deeper insights into the one will have a similar impact on the other.

THE PILGRIM'S EARLY ATTEMPTS TO ANSWER HIS QUESTION

Summary

The author's experience at the liturgy gives rise to the fundamental question of his spiritual journey: What does the apostle mean by the words "pray without ceasing"? In this section of his narrative, he describes his initial attempts to understand the meaning of this puzzling phrase: (1) he checks the Bible himself, (2) goes to different churches to see if anything is preached about it, and (3) seeks an explanation from an experienced and knowledgeable guide. We look at each of these individually, in the following paragraphs.

1. These early attempts to discover the truth about the apostle's words serve to increase rather than satisfy the Pilgrim's hunger for

the truth. He opens his Bible and reads with his own eyes "...that we ought always, at all times and in all places, to pray with uplifted hands."[7] This exhortation is a common theme in Paul's writings (see 1 Thess 5:17; Eph 6:18; 1 Tim 2:8) and assures him that he has not been imagining things. The words themselves, however, do not bring him understanding. Their meaning remains closed to his eyes, and he realizes that he needs someone to explain them to him.

2. When he visits some of the churches that were known for their good preachers, he hears many sermons about the nature, need, and fruits of prayer, but nothing specifically on how to *succeed* at prayer. He listens to one preacher speak about interior and ceaseless prayer, but finds him too abstract and with nothing to say about the practical steps one can take to attain such a prayer. Tired of listening to such sermons geared to a general audience, the Pilgrim eventually decides to look elsewhere for answers to his questions.

3. At this point, the idea finally comes to him to ask an experienced and knowledgeable guide about the meaning of the apostle's words. With Bible in hand, he travels for a long time in search of an experienced guide who can help him. In one village, he meets a gentleman who has a chapel in his house and who devotes a great deal of time to prayer and spiritual reading. When asked about the apostle's words, he looks closely at the impoverished Pilgrim and responds:

> Ceaseless interior prayer is a continual yearning of the human spirit toward God. To succeed in this consoling exercise we must pray more often to God to teach us to pray without ceasing. Pray more, and pray more fervently. It is prayer itself which will reveal to you how it can be achieved unceasingly; but it will take some time.[8]

The Pilgrim accepts the gentleman's hospitality but is not satisfied with his response. He is interested in the actual particulars of unceasing prayer, not some general advice about praying with more fervor. And so he continues his search.

He covers about a hundred and twenty-five miles when he meets the abbot of a monastery in a large provincial capital. When asked about the meaning of unceasing prayer, the monk takes out *The Spiritual Education of the Inner Man* by Saint Dmitri and shows him that the apostle's words refer to "the creative prayer of the understanding,"[9] which can always reach out to God and pray without ceasing. But when asked to explain what Saint Dmitri means by such prayer, this holy abbot can offer nothing more than that "[i]t is very difficult, even for one to whom God himself gives such a gift."[10] Once again, the Pilgrim is not satisfied with the response. He spends the night in the monastery and continues his journey the next day with no idea whatsoever where he is headed.

Reflection

These initial steps taken to satisfy the Pilgrim's spiritual query reveal a lot about the quest for spiritual guidance. For one thing, the Bible stands out as the normative rule of life that promises to guide the Pilgrim and lead him to the truth. He goes out of his way to verify what he has heard, finds other texts from Scripture to back up its claim, and enjoys reading the Bible at every stage of his wanderings. Reading the Bible is one of the constants of his spiritual journey. What he needs is someone to help him interpret it, especially the cryptic words of the apostle in 1 Thessalonians 5:17.

In search of such clarification, the Pilgrim turns to the official proclamation of the Word in the churches, but finds that the sermons are geared toward a much wider audience. When he finally decides to consult an experienced spiritual guide, he discovers that this, too, is a difficult and arduous task. Despite these setbacks, the Pilgrim does not lose hope; the more obstacles he encounters in his search, the more determined he becomes to discover the meaning of unceasing prayer.

When it comes to the search for spiritual guidance, the experiences of the Pilgrim on this leg of his journey encourage us to examine, first of all, our own attitude toward the sacred Scriptures.

Do we truly believe that Scripture contains the revelation of God to humanity? If so, then in what sense? Does the Bible form a part of our daily spiritual reading? If not, why? Do we, like the Pilgrim, ponder the words that seem shrouded in mystery? Do we make any attempt to understand them?

When going through the Pilgrim's early attempts to satisfy his spiritual query, we should also be encouraged to examine our own attitude toward the Church's official proclamation of the Word of God. Although it is true that the Pilgrim does not find the answers to his questions in the sermons he hears, it is also true that he thinks enough of them to go and listen to them with an attentive ear. Can we say the same for our own experience of the proclaimed Word of God? Do we expect to receive guidance from the words proclaimed from the pulpit? Do we understand that attentive listening to the proclaimed Word of God is just as important (if not more) as its careful preparation and execution? Although the Pilgrim eventually gives up on sermons geared toward the general public, because they do not meet his particular spiritual needs, he still has a high regard for the role they play in the ongoing spiritual formation of the Christian faithful. For the Pilgrim, the sermon's important role in spiritual guidance of ordinary Christians never comes into question. Can we make the same claim?

Finally, when we see the Pilgrim continuing his journey after so many disappointments, we should be encouraged never to lose heart. This holds true especially when it comes to finding a competent spiritual director who is able to answer our questions and satisfy our spiritual needs. In his early attempts to find a spiritual guide able to explain to him the meaning of the apostle's words, the Pilgrim encounters a member of the landed gentry and a saintly abbot, each of whom is extremely hospitable and sincere in wanting to help him come to a deeper understanding of 1 Thessalonians 5:17. Neither, however, is sufficiently equipped to satisfy his deep and ardent desire to understand and practice unceasing prayer. The Pilgrim must travel many miles and suffer many disappointments before he finds a director capable of helping him. When it comes to finding the right spiritual director to meet our needs, we must be ready to suffer disappointments and wait patiently until the right one comes along.

THE PILGRIM'S RELATIONSHIP WITH HIS STARETS

Until now, the Pilgrim has made little progress in his attempt to understand the meaning of unceasing prayer. As he continues his journey, he grieves over his ill-fortune and comforts himself by reading the holy Bible. He journeys for five days along the main road when, late one afternoon, toward evening, an old man comes up to him and engages him in conversation. The Pilgrim unburdens his heart to the old man, who turns out to be a monk from a nearby hermitage who winds up talking to him about deep spiritual matters. The old man eventually becomes the Pilgrim's *starets* (spiritual father), the one who will explain to him the meaning of unceasing prayer and introduce him to the practice of the Jesus Prayer. It is not without significance that it is the *starets* who finds the Pilgrim— and not vice versa. The answer to the Pilgrim's spiritual query comes to him when he least expects it.

At this point, the narrative can be divided into four parts: (1) the Pilgrim and the monk's journey together on the road, (2) their conversation in the *starets'* cell, (3) their summer discussions, and (4) the death of the *starets* and the Pilgrim's departure. For purposes of continuity and exposition, the summary and reflection sections are combined for the next four sections.

The Pilgrim and the Monk Journey Together: Summary and Reflection
The relationship between the Pilgrim and his *starets* offers some interesting lessons about the dynamics of spiritual direction. As they

are walking along the road, the old man looks out for the Pilgrim's physical needs by inviting him to go with him to his hermitage and receive the hospitality of his community. The Pilgrim is reluctant to go and comments that he has more need for spiritual guidance than for shelter. The monk persists, stating that there are experienced elders in his monastery who can nourish him spiritually.

As they make their way to the hermitage, the Pilgrim then feels free to share his story. The old monk listens attentively to all that the Pilgrim has to say about his deep burning desire to understand what it means to pray without ceasing, and about his disappointment in not being able to find a satisfactory explanation. When the Pilgrim finishes, the elder monk makes the Sign of the Cross and gives thanks to God for having given the Pilgrim this irresistible longing to acquire unceasing interior prayer. He tells the Pilgrim that he must recognize the call of God in this longing. What is more, he explains, the Pilgrim must understand that his disappointing experiences were God's providential way of telling him that the divine illumination of unceasing interior prayer is not reached by the wisdom of this world nor mere superficial curiosity. Rather, "…it is found in poverty of spirit and in active experience in simplicity of heart."[11]

The monk goes on to say that he is not surprised that the Pilgrim had so much difficulty in understanding the meaning of the apostle's words. Many preachers, he states, talk about what constitutes prayer than about its essence; they base their sermons on speculation rather than on living experience; they lack the mystical experience that goes beyond mere academic knowledge. Many people, moreover, put the cart before the horse when it comes to prayer; they mistakenly think that it is the effort one makes and the preparatory steps one takes that give rise to prayer, rather than prayer giving rise to good works and virtuous living. In his mind, "[t]hose who reason so take, incorrectly, the fruits and the results of prayer for the means of attaining it, and this is to depreciate the power of prayer."[12] The *starets* quotes Scripture (see 1 Tim 2:1; Rom 8:26) and Saint Isaac the Syrian to point out that prayer comes before good works. He also states that "…the perfection of prayer does not lie within our power."[13] Realizing that he was in the presence of a deeply spiritual and knowledgeable man, the Pilgrim asks the *starets* to explain the meaning of unceasing prayer and how one can learn it. By this time, they have arrived at the monastery. The *starets* invites the Pilgrim to enter his cell where they can continue their discussion.

Even in his initial dealings with the Pilgrim, the *starets* displays many of the most important qualities to look for in a good spiritual director: concern for the physical well-being of others, creating an atmosphere where others feel free to share their life's story, attentive listening, the recognition of a call, a reasonable interpretation of past experiences in light of God's providential care, drawing the distinction between speculative and experiential knowledge, insight into the essence of prayer, drawing out prayer's important significance for the moral life, recognizing the role of grace in the spiritual life. Of all the qualities to look for, the most important, probably, is to find someone who is willing to journey with the directee, evidenced in this instance by the long five-mile walk to the hermitage that the two men make as they discuss matters pertaining to the spiritual life.

In the Starets' *Cell: Summary and Reflection*

Once in the cell, the *starets* goes into more detail about how to learn and practice unceasing prayer. He begins with a clear instruction about its nature and scope.

> The continuous interior Prayer of Jesus is a constant uninterrupted calling upon the divine name of Jesus with the lips, in the spirit, in the heart; while forming a mental picture of his constant presence, and imploring his grace, during every occupation, at all times, in all places, even during sleep. The appeal is couched in these terms, "Lord Jesus

Christ, have mercy on me." One who accustoms himself to this appeal experiences as a result so deep a consolation and so great a need to offer the Prayer always, that he can no longer live without it, and it will continue to voice itself within him of its own accord.[14]

The *starets* does not mince words or beat around the bush. He goes straight to the heart of the matter and, in the process, gives the Pilgrim the clearest explanation he has yet received about the meaning of unceasing prayer. The *starets'* clarity of expression is a reminder to all spiritual directors that they should speak to their directees in a simple, unassuming manner. They should try to use language in such a way that they speak the truth clearly and yet, at the same time, touch the depths of the heart.

The Pilgrim is impressed by the *starets'* words. When asked if he now understands the meaning of unceasing prayer, he responds: "Yes indeed, Father, and in God's name teach me how to gain the habit of it!"[15]

Now comes what is probably one of the most crucial moments of their conversation, for it is at this point that the *starets* introduces the Pilgrim to *The Philokalia*, a collection of the writings of twenty-five holy Fathers which "...contains the full and detailed science of constant interior prayer."[16] The humility of the *starets* comes through in this one sweeping gesture. He does not pretend to have all the answers himself. Rather, he points the Pilgrim to one of the primary sources of his own knowledge of the spiritual life. To be sure, he himself claims that "...it is considered the foremost and best manual of the contemplative spiritual life."[17] By pointing the Pilgrim to this masterful book of spiritual guidance, the *starets* humbly admits his own limitations as a spiritual guide and points the Pilgrim to a reputable and highly respected source of the Christian tradition. Spiritual directors must, in the same way, recognize their limitations in the relationship of spiritual direction. The skill they must seek to develop is not that of having all the answers, but of helping their directees look into the tradition and listen to it. Much of the rest of the Pilgrim's story is about the gradual process whereby he became more and more immersed in the tradition of *The Philokalia*.

The *starets* has barely introduced the Pilgrim to this holy book when he faces another important question: "Is it then more sublime and holy than the Bible?"[18] Once again, the *starets* uses clarity of expression and imagery that touches the heart to make his point. In the first place, the *Philokalia* is not holier than the Bible, but contains enlightened explanations of the Bible that shortsighted minds cannot easily attain. He uses the image of a viewing lens to make his point.

> The sun is the greatest, the most resplendent, and the most wonderful of heavenly luminaries, but you cannot contemplate and examine it simply with unprotected eyes. You have to use a piece of artificial glass which is many millions of times smaller and darker than the sun. But through this little piece of glass you can examine the magnificent monarch of the stars, delight in it, and endure its fiery rays. Holy Scripture also is a dazzling sun, and this book, *The Philokalia*, is the piece of glass which we use to enable us to contemplate the sun in its imperial splendor.[19]

The *starets* then opens *The Philokalia* and reads to him passages from Saint Simeon the New Theologian, Saint Gregory of Sinai, Saint Callistus, and Saint Ignatius, all of which supply practical instructions about how to begin praying the Jesus Prayer. The Pilgrim is thoroughly fascinated with what the *starets* lays out before him. He listens attentively and tries to remember as much as he possibly can. They spend the entire night absorbed in holy conversation—and then go off to matins.

The *starets* knows *The Philokalia* so well that he is able to open it and find just the right passages that will move the Pilgrim's heart. Like any good spiritual director, he meets the Pilgrim where he is and takes care not to provide him with spiritual counsel that he does not understand or is too far over his head. As a result, the Pilgrim's life is irrevocably changed. This one chance meeting on the road-side leads to a wealth of spiritual treasure for him, and he is deter-mined not to let it slip away. He knows for certain that he has finally found someone who will teach him the way of unceasing prayer. In the remainder of the first narrative, the Pilgrim gives a step-by-step account of this learning process.

The Pilgrim and the Monk Deepen Their Spiritual Relationship: Summary and Reflection

By the time they part after matins, the *starets* and the Pilgrim have a well-established relationship of spiritual guidance. They have jour-neyed together, listened to each other, recognized the Pilgrim's call to unceasing prayer, and resolved to do something about that call. The *starets* instructs the Pilgrim to visit him frequently and to confess his sins to him openly and honestly, "…for the inward process could not go on properly and successfully without the guidance of a teacher."[20]

The *starets* is clearly willing to assume this role of director; he also realizes that spiritual direction involves the directee's complete and total honesty with the director. The confession of sin, for the *starets*, is intricately tied to the process of direction. It is impossible to make progress toward God if we are not at the same time exam-ining ourselves and confronting the darkness that lives in the soul and manifests itself in concrete deeds and attitudes. Today, those spiritual directors who draw a sharp distinction between direction and confession must at least make clear to their directees that direc-tion is not a substitute for the confession of sins, and that they still need to confront the darkness in their lives in a visible and concrete way.

As the narrative continues, we discover how the Pilgrim over-comes some practical difficulties. He experiences a deep, burning zeal to learn unceasing prayer as quickly as possible, but wonders how he can do this when the monastery where the *starets* resides has a three-day limit for guests and there are no other residences in the vicinity. He resolves this difficulty by finding work and lodging for the summer in a small village some three miles away. This gives him the opportunity to be near his *starets* and to apply himself to the regimen he sets for himself.

In like manner, the relationship of spiritual direction demands a certain amount of regularity, especially in its initial stages. This means, on the one hand, that the director must be willing to meet frequently with the directee and be careful not to take on more directees than he or she is able to manage at any one time. On the other hand, it requires the directee to make appropriate adjustments so that he or she will be able to enjoy the benefits of the director, either through direct visits, letters, or other viable means.

As the Pilgrim settles down in his new dwelling, he eagerly sets out to do all that the *starets* has taught him about the Jesus Prayer, making sure that he visits him from time to time. It is here where we see the dynamics of the spiritual direction unfold. All goes well at first, as the Pilgrim works in a secluded garden and tries to implement the teaching of the *starets*. After about a week, however, he begins to feel lazy, bored, sleepy, and distracted by disturbing thoughts. The *starets* tells him that this is the kingdom of darkness waging war against him and that the enemy will try to do anything to thwart him in his attempt to pray without ceasing.

The *starets* concludes that the Pilgrim has tried to delve too quickly into the prayer of the heart, and refers him to a passage of the Blessed Nicephorus the Solitary in *The Philokalia,* which speaks precisely about this difficulty. The solution is to begin reciting the Jesus Prayer many times a day with the lips, increasing the number until the words become so much a part of him that he will one day not need to utter them physically because they will come directly and unceasingly from the heart.

At this point in the process, two elements of the spiritual dynamic stand out. In the first place, the Pilgrim is *completely* honest with the *starets* about his experience at prayer. This is a *sine qua non* for spiritual direction. The more directees tend to hold something back from their director about their relationship to God, the less they will benefit from their director's guidance. It is important that the director and the directee address issues of honesty from the outset of their relationship. If this does not occur, the relationship of direction will become contrived and unauthentic.

In the second place, the directors must determine how far along a directee has progressed in his or her relationship to God and be able to provide appropriate spiritual counsel that will meet that person's spiritual needs. In the case of the Pilgrim, the *starets* recognizes that he is trying to do too much in too little time. He therefore slows him down in his attempt to reach the experience of unceasing prayer, and does so with practical, concrete instructions: he gives the Pilgrim a *chotki* (a prayer rope or rosary), tells him to follow his exact instructions and, over a period of time, tells him to recite the Jesus Prayer with his lips only, first three thousand times daily; then, after two days, six thousand times daily; then, after ten days, twelve thousand times daily; and eventually as often as he so desires. Only until the recitation of prayer becomes a deeply rooted habit in the Pilgrim's daily routine does the *starets* give the Pilgrim permission to cease praying with the lips. He allows this because, all the while, the Prayer has been gradually making its way into his heart.

All during this time, the Pilgrim listens attentively to his spiritual father's instructions and takes great pains to carry them out. As a result, he is blessed with an ever-increasing desire to pray the Jesus Prayer and discovers, much to his amazement, that the prayer of the lips becomes easier and easier to say throughout the day. In time, he becomes less and less reliant on this outward structure of prayer. Because he is honest with his director, attentively listens, and carries out his instructions, the Pilgrim is able to internalize the Prayer and make it an integral part of his interior life. Frequent visits, honesty, attentive listening and action (for example, obedience) help facilitate the gradual interiorization of the structures of the spiritual life, which the *starets* uses to shape the soul of his directee. The *starets*, moreover, helps the Pilgrim understand the various physical, emotional, mental, and spiritual effects of the Jesus Prayer: it brings a burning sensation to the heart; it purifies the passions; it brings clarity of mind and purity of heart.

The Pilgrim accepts this guidance for the entire summer, working alone in the nearby village, repeating the Jesus Prayer with his lips and, in the process, finding that his experiences of time, place, even people begin to change: the long monastic service appears so short; his solitary hut seems like a magnificent palace; without exception, everyone he meets appears dear to him. What's more, conscious of his sinfulness, he is grateful to God for bringing him into contact with the holy *starets*. This one man has been an instrument of God who helps bring about a change of vision in the life of the Pilgrim.

Death and Departure: Summary and Reflection

As the summer draws to an close, this holy man becomes ill and dies, but not before giving the Pilgrim his blessing and allowing him to keep the *chotki* (rosary) as a keepsake. With the death of his director and the end of his summer job, the Pilgrim is now free to continue his journey. It is not surprising that he buys a beat-up copy of *The Philokalia* with the two roubles that he has earned from his summer work. With the death of his *starets*, this book becomes, apart from the Bible, the primary source of spiritual nourishment in his life. Indeed, the rest of the story tells of how the Pilgrim internalizes the book's teachings (the new spiritual structure in his life) and imparts the wealth of his experience to others. It is, in other words, the story of his journey to become a *starets* (that is, a spiritual father) for those he encounters along life's journey.

CONCLUSION

In the four movements of the first narrative, the anonymous Pilgrim author sheds a great deal of light on the importance of competent guidance in the spiritual life. His honest estimation of himself in the eyes of God and his fellow human beings, the origins of his spiritual query, his early attempts to satisfy it, and the relationship with his *starets* demonstrate some of the difficulties we, ourselves, can encounter in the search for competent spiritual direction. At the end of this narrative, one of the most important qualities that stands out in the Pilgrim's search for the meaning of unceasing prayer is his refusal to accept answers that fail to satisfy both heart *and* mind and his dogged persistence, in the midst of great difficulty, not to give up looking for the spiritual guidance he know he needs.

At the end of this first narrative, the Pilgrim is in an advantageous position for realizing his dream of unceasing prayer. After some initial disappointments, he finds a spiritual guide who is willing to take him under his wing and introduce him to the mysteries of this enigmatic form of prayer. In the space of a few months, the Pilgrim benefits from the insights of this *starets* and may very well have been the last person to be instructed by the man before his death.

Under his spiritual director, the Pilgrim learns the rudiments of unceasing prayer and is introduced to *The Philokalia* as the guide *par excellence* of the spiritual life—the guide that will accompany him throughout the rest of his spiritual journey. His relationship with his *starets* is so close that he will even have experiences of him after the man's death—in dreams, visions, and moments of intuition.

The first narrative of *The Way of a Pilgrim* points out the difficulties involved in getting started in the spiritual life and entering into a firmly established relationship of spiritual direction. With the death of the *starets*, the first narrative also points to the transitory nature of that relationship and celebrates the larger hand that Providence most certainly plays in the daily lives of believers and nonbelievers alike. As the Pilgrim continues his journey, he has added one important piece of baggage to his scant collection of belongings: *The Philokalia*. He leaves his *starets* behind but takes the man's spirit with him, as it is represented in print in the wisdom of this holy book. The Pilgrim has finally found that all-important lens with which to view Scripture (especially 1 Thess 5:17) and ponder its meaning. Just how this invaluable instrument will guide him is a matter not only for him but also for God to decide.

REFLECTION QUESTIONS

1. Do you, like the Pilgrim, have a sense of a call or purpose in life? How would you describe that call or purpose? How does it manifest itself in your daily life? What does it have to do with your vision and outlook on life? How does it affect your relationships with material possessions? with others? with God? Has this sense of call or purpose changed over the years? What is it presently asking you to do with your life? What is it asking of you for the future? How would you like it to develop?

2. Do you find it easy to consider your life in terms of a pilgrimage? Where have you wandered through the years? Did you ever feel as though it has been an aimless wandering without sense or direction? Have you ever felt as though you were being led by someone? If so, by whom or what? What is the goal of your journey through life? Do you think you will ever get there? If so, how?

3. Like the Pilgrim's experience of 1 Thessalonians 5:17 on the twenty-fourth Sunday after Pentecost, have you ever been struck by a particular verse from Scripture? Which one(s)? How did it occur? Where were you? What were you doing? How did you react to it? Did it stay with you for quite some time? How did it inspire you? What did it prompt you to do? Did you do it? Can you think of

other instances in your life when you were inspired by the Word of God present in Scripture? in creation? in the words of a sage?

4. What other attempts have you made to understand the meaning of God's Word for you? Do you read the Bible? Do you pray over it? Do you listen to the sermons at church? Do you ponder them? Have you sought out a knowledgeable guide to help you understand the ways of prayer and to what God is calling you in life? In what ways have you been disappointed or frustrated in your quest? In what ways have you been surprised? Have you ever lost heart? In what other ways do you actively seek to understand God's will for you in your life?

5. What does prayer mean to you? Does your own prayer give rise to good works and virtuous living in your life—or vice versa? Do you pray in different ways? If so, how? Do you pray with your body? with your mind? with your emotions? with your spirit? Do you pray with others? Do you pray alone? How would you describe the rhythm of prayer that you have acquired over the years? Is it a good, healthy rhythm? What are its weaknesses? In what ways could it be improved?

6. What do you understand by the apostle Paul's exhortation in 1 Thessalonians 5:17, "to pray without ceasing?" Do you think it is possible? Have you ever felt as though you were praying throughout the day? during the night? during your sleep? What do you make of the Jesus Prayer? Does it appeal to you? What do you like about it? What don't you like about it? Is it an integral part of your prayer life? Do you want it to be? What keeps you from making it so?

7. What do you understand by spiritual direction? How do you understand the director/directee relationship? Should a spiritual director be directive? non-directive? a companion for you on your spiritual journey? How would you describe the relationship between

the Pilgrim and his *starets*? Is it a type of relationship you would like to have? What are its positive elements? negative elements?

8. What are the qualities you look for in a good spiritual director? Have you ever had trouble finding a spiritual director? How do you know if a spiritual director is actually helping you? Have you ever been disappointed by a spiritual director? If so, how did you handle the situation? Have you been honest with your directors—completely honest? Have your spiritual directors entered your life by chance? circumstance? the hand of God?

9. Do you consider yourself, like the Pilgrim, to be a proponent of a particular school of spirituality? If so, how does that spirituality manifest itself in the concrete circumstances of your life? If you are more eclectic in your spiritual outlook, how do you go about deciding which elements suit you and which do not? How do you share your spirituality with others? Have you ever found yourself in a position where *you* were helping someone in *their* life of prayer?

10. The Pilgrim has a strong relationship with his *starets*, one that goes beyond death and focuses on the teaching of *The Philokalia*. Where are the strong relationships in your life, those that carry through life—and beyond? Like *The Philokalia*, is there a particular book or set of spiritual teachings that provide for you the lens through which you meditate and ponder the mysteries of God's Word? Try to be as specific as possible.

EXERCISES

1. Find a quiet place where you can be alone with yourself and God for twenty to thirty minutes. Close your eyes and breathe deeply—in and out. Recite the words of the Jesus Prayer on your lips, to the rhythm of your breathing, and then slowly to the beating

of your heart. Then let the words move slowly from your lips to your mind and then to your heart. Focus on nothing but the words, and let them carry you into the depths of your spirit. Rest there in the Lord for as long as you like. At the end of the period, ask the Lord to help you call on his holy name at all times, especially when the pace of life gets hectic and the path you should take is difficult to discern. If you feel up to it, repeat the process a second time.

2. Go over Narrative I of *The Way of a Pilgrim*. Try to put yourself in the place of the wandering Pilgrim. Follow him in your mind as he enters the church and is struck by Paul's words to "pray without ceasing." Go with the Pilgrim in his search for the meaning of these words. Stay with him during his early disappointments until he meets his *starets* and is introduced to the Jesus Prayer and the mysteries of *The Philokalia*. As you read the narrative, try to be conscious of your feelings and thoughts, as well as the movement of your heart. See if there are any similarities between the Pilgrim's spiritual journey and your own.

3. Take out some paper (your journal, if you keep one) and write the story of your prayer life. Be as honest and specific as possible, including your difficulties as well as your triumphs. Write your first remembrance of prayer, the forms you preferred when you were a child, the ones you adopted as you grew older, the ones you employ now. Include in your narration those people who helped you learn to pray: a parent, a teacher, a close friend, a priest or minister. Include also those moments in your life when you helped someone along the way of prayer.

When you have finished writing your story, read it over and ask yourself what is unique about it. Is there a certain difficulty, a particular theme, or a pressing problem that runs throughout? How would you summarize the story of your life of prayer? If there is someone you would feel comfortable sharing it with (your spiritual director), do so. Is there anything keeping you from sharing your story with another?

4. Put an hour aside for a leisurely walk. Have a particular destination in mind, but don't necessarily plan on getting there. Before you leave on this brief spiritual pilgrimage, ask the Lord to help you to be particularly aware of the people whose paths you will cross along the way. Start out at a pace that you feel comfortable with. Take a prayer rope or a rosary with you to finger gently as you pray the Jesus Prayer over and over according to the rhythm of your gait. Walk with a sense of gratitude for the simplest gifts God has given you: your life, your health, the ability to breathe and to walk. As you walk, direct you attention to all those you pass. Pray for each person individually. Ask God to bless each person with a deeper sense of the divine presence within. When you return, go to a quiet place and think about all the ways in which God has spoken to you during the last hour.

5. Look back at the end of the day, and make a list of all that has occurred. Write or simply list in your mind all the situations—major and minor—that you found yourself in throughout the day. Ask yourself where God was in each situation. Did God seem present? absent? actively involved? a detached observer? In what ways did you help or hinder the spread of the gospel in each situation?

Did you find yourself praying during the day? Did you feel as though you were praying always? Did you honestly try to offer God your participation in the events of the day? What mistakes did you make? How could you do better? Did you remember to ask God for help? Even if you were not consciously thinking of God, was your spirit in union with God's Spirit? Did you call upon the holy name of Jesus throughout the day? Did you pray the Jesus Prayer? often? seldom? not at all?

When you have finished this examination of the events of the day, thank God for all that has happened, and ask for the grace to respond with a more open and loving heart.

Narrative II
The Way of a Pilgrim

༈

I wandered about for a long time in different districts, having for my fellow traveler the Prayer of Jesus, which heartened and consoled me in all my journeys, in all my meetings with other people, and in all the happenings of travel.

But I came to feel at last that it would be better for me to stay in some one place in order to be alone more often so as to be able to keep by myself and study *The Philokalia*. Although I read it whenever I found shelter for the night or rested during the day, yet I greatly wished to go more and more deeply into it and, with faith and heartfelt prayer, to learn from its teaching about the truth for the salvation of my soul.

However, in spite of all my wishes, I could nowhere find any work that I was able to do, for I had lost the use of my left arm when quite a child. Seeing that because of this I should not be able to get myself a fixed abode, I made up my mind to go into Siberia to the tomb of Saint Innocent of Irkutsk. My idea was that in the forests and steppes of Siberia I should travel in greater silence and, therefore, in a way that was better for prayer and reading. And this journey I undertook, all the while saying my oral Prayer without stopping.

After no great lapse of time, I had the feeling that the Prayer had, so to speak, by its own action, passed from my lips to my heart. That is to say, it seemed as though my heart in its ordinary beating began to say the words of the Prayer within at each beat. Thus, for example, *one,* "Lord," *two,* "Jesus," *three,* "Christ," and so on. I gave up saying the Prayer with my lips. I simply listened carefully to what my heart was saying. It seemed as though my eyes looked right down into it; and I dwelled upon the words of my departed *starets* when he was telling me about this joy.

Then I felt something like a slight pain in my heart, and in my thoughts so great a love for Jesus Christ that I pictured myself, if only I could see him, throwing myself at his feet and not letting them go from my embrace, kissing them tenderly, and thanking him with tears for having, of his love and grace, allowed me to find so great a consolation in his name—me, his unworthy and sinful creature! Further, there came into my heart a gracious warmth which spread through my whole breast. This moved me to a still closer reading of *The Philokalia* in order to test my feelings and to make a thorough study of the business of secret prayer in the heart. For without such testing I was afraid of falling a victim to the mere charm of it, or of taking natural effects for the effects of grace, and of giving way to pride at my quick learning of the Prayer. It was of this danger that I had heard my departed *starets* speak.

For this reason, I took to walking more by night and chose to spend my days reading *The Philokalia,* sitting down under a tree in the forest. Ah! what wisdom, such as I had never known before, was shown me by this reading! Giving myself up to it, I felt a delight which till then I had never been able to imagine. It is true that many places were still beyond the grasp of my dull mind. But my prayer in the heart brought with it the clearing up of things I did not understand. Sometimes also, though very rarely, I saw my departed *starets* in a dream, and he threw light upon many things and, most of all, guided my ignorant soul more and more toward humility.

In this blissful state I passed more than two months of the summer. For the most part I went through the forests and along bypaths.

When I came to a village I asked only for a bag of dried bread and a handful of salt. I filled my bark jar with water and so, on for another sixty miles or so.

Toward the end of the summer, temptation began to attack me, perhaps as a result of the sins on my wretched soul; perhaps as something needed in the spiritual life; perhaps as the best way of giving me teaching and experience. A clear case in point was the following. One day when I came out on to the main road as twilight was falling, two men with shaved heads who looked like a couple of soldiers came up to me. They demanded money. When I told them that I had not a penny on me, they would not believe me and shouted insolently, "You're lying. Pilgrims always pick up lots of money."

"What's the good of arguing with him!" said one of them, and gave me such a blow on the head with his oak cudgel that I dropped senseless. I do not know whether I remained senseless long but when I came to, I found myself lying in the forest by the roadside, robbed. My knapsack had gone; all that was left of it were the cords from which it hung, which they had cut. Thank God they had not stolen my passport, which I carried in my old fur cap so as to be able to show it as quickly as possible on demand. I got up weeping bitterly, not so much on account of the pain in my head as for the loss of my books, the Bible and *The Philokalia,* which were in the stolen knapsack.

Day and night I did not cease to weep and lament. Where was it now, my Bible which I had always carried with me and which I had always read from my youth onwards? Where was my *Philokalia,* from which I had gained so much teaching and consolation? How unhappy I was to have lost the first and last treasures of my life before having had my fill of them! It would have been better to be killed outright than to live without this spiritual food. For I should never be able to replace the books now.

For two days I just dragged myself along. I was so crushed by the weight of my misfortune and, on the third, I quite reached the end of my strength and, dropping down in the shelter of a bush, I fell asleep. And then I had a dream. I was back at the monastery in the cell of my *starets,* deploring my loss. The old man was trying to comfort me. He said, "Let this be a lesson to you in detachment from earthly things for your better advance toward heaven. This has been allowed to happen to you to save you from falling into the mere enjoyment of spiritual things. God would have the Christian absolutely renounce all his desires and delights and attachments, and to submit himself entirely to his divine will. He orders every event for the help and salvation of man; *He wills that all men should be saved.* Take courage then and believe that God *will, with the temptation, provide also a way of escape* (1 Cor 10:13). Soon you will be rejoicing much more than you are now distressed." At these words I awoke, feeling my strength come back to me and my soul full of light and peace. "God's will be done," I said. I crossed myself, got up and went on my way. The Prayer again began to be active in my heart, as before, and for three days I went along in peace.

All at once I came upon a body of convicts with their military escort. When I came up to them I recognized the two men who had robbed me. They were in the outside file, and so I fell at their feet and earnestly begged them to tell me what they had done with my books. At first, they paid no heed to me, but in the end one of them said, "If you will give us something we will tell you where your books are. Give us a rouble." I swore to them that even if I had to beg the rouble from someone for the love of God, I would certainly give it to them, and by way of pledge I offered them my passport. Then they told me that my books were in the wagons which followed the prisoners, among all the other stolen things they were found with.

"How can I get them?"

"Ask the officer in charge of us."

I hurried to the officer and told him the whole story.

"Can you really read the Bible?" he asked me.

"Yes," I answered, "not only can I read everything, but what is more, I can write, too. You will see a signature in the Bible which shows it is mine, and here is my passport showing the same name and surname."

He then told me that the rascals who had robbed me were deserters living in a mud hut in the forest and that they had plundered many people, but that a clever driver whose *troika* they had tried to steal had captured them the day before. "All right," he added, "I will give you your books back if they are there, but you come with us as far as our halting place for the night; it is only a little over two miles, then I need not stop the whole convoy and the wagons just for your sake." I agreed to this gladly and, as I walked along at his horse's side, we began to talk.

I saw that he was a kindly and honest fellow and no longer young. He asked me who I was, where I came from, and where I was going. I answered all his questions without hiding anything, and so we reached the house which marked the end of the day's march. He found my books and gave them back to me, saying, "Where are you going now that night has come? Stay here and sleep in my anteroom." So I stayed.

Now that I had my books again, I was so glad that I did not know how to thank God. I clasped the books to my breast and held them there so long that my hands got quite numbed. I shed tears of joy and my heart beat with delight. The officer watched me and said, "You must love reading your Bible very much!" But such was my joy that I could not answer him; I could only weep. Then he went on to say, "I also read the Gospel regularly every day, Brother." He produced a small copy of the Gospels, printed in Kiev and bound in silver, saying, "Sit down, and I will tell you how it came about."

"Let us have some supper," he said.

We drew up to the table and the officer began his story.

"Ever since I was a young man I have been with the army in the field and not on garrison service. I knew my job, and my superior officers liked me for a conscientious second lieutenant. Still, I was young and so were my friends. Unhappily, I took to drink, and drunkenness became a regular passion with me. So long as I kept away from drink, I was a good officer, but when I gave way to it, I was no good for anything for six weeks at a time. They bore with me for a long while, but the end of it was that after being thoroughly rude while drunk to my commanding officer, I was cashiered and transferred to a garrison as a private soldier for three years. I was threatened with a still more severe punishment if I did not give up drinking and mend my ways.

"Even in this miserable state of affairs, however much I tried, I could not regain my self-control nor cure myself. I found it impossible to get rid of my passion for drink, and it was decided to send me to a disciplinary corps. When I was informed of this, I was at my wit's end. I was in barracks occupied with my wretched thoughts when there arrived a monk who was going round collecting for a church. We each of us gave him what we could.

"He came up to me and asked me why I was so unhappy, and I talked to him and told him my troubles. He sympathized with me and said, 'The same thing happened to my own brother, and what do you think helped him? His spiritual father gave him a copy of the Gospels with strict orders to read a chapter without a moment's delay every time he felt a longing for wine coming over him. If the desire continued he was to read a second chapter, and so on. That is what my brother did and, at the end of a very short time, his drunkenness came to an end. It is now fifteen years since he touched a drop of alcohol. You do the same and you will see how that will help you. I have a copy of the Gospels which you must let me bring you.'

"I listened to him, and then I said, 'How can your Gospels help me since all efforts of my own and all the medical treatment have failed to stop me drinking?' I talked in that way because I had as yet never been in the habit of reading the Gospels. 'Don't say that,' replied the monk, 'I assure you that it will be a help.' As a matter of fact, the next day he brought me this very copy. I opened it, took a glance, and said, 'I cannot accept it. I am not used to Church Slavonic and don't understand it.' But the monk went on to assure me that in the very words of the Gospel there lay a gracious power, for in them was written what God himself had spoken. 'It does not matter very much if at first you do not understand, go on reading diligently. A monk once said, "If you do not understand the Word of God, the devils understand what you are reading, and tremble," and your drunkenness is certainly the work of devils. And here is another thing I will tell you. Saint John Chrysostom writes that even a room in which a copy of the Gospels is kept holds the spirits of darkness at bay, and becomes an unpromising field for their wiles.'

"I forget what I gave the monk. But I bought his book of the Gospels, put it away in a trunk with my other things, and forgot it. Some while afterwards, a bout of drunkenness threatened me. An irresistible desire for drink drove me hurriedly to open my trunk to get some money and rush off to the public house. But the first thing my eyes fell on was the copy of the Gospels, and all that the monk had said came back vividly to my mind. I opened the book and began to read the first chapter of Saint Matthew. I got to the end of it without understanding a word. Still, I remembered that the monk had said, 'No matter if you do not understand, go on reading diligently.'

"'Come,' said I, 'I must read the second chapter.' I did so and began to understand a little. So I started on the third chapter and then the barracks bell began to ring; everyone had to go to bed, no one was allowed to go out, and I had to stay where I was. When I got up in the morning I was just on the point of going out to get some wine when I suddenly thought—supposing I were to read another chapter? What would be the result? I read it and I did not go to the public house. Again I felt the craving and again I read a chapter. I felt a certain amount of relief. This encouraged me and, from that time on, whenever I felt the need of drink, I used to read a chapter of the Gospels. What is more, as time went on, things got better and better, and by the time I had finished all four Gospels my drunkenness was absolutely a thing of the past, and I felt nothing but disgust for it. It is just twenty years now since I drank a drop of alcohol.

"Everybody was astonished at the change brought about in me. Some three years later my commission was restored to me. In due course I was promoted and finally got my majority. I married; I am blessed with a good wife. We have made a position for ourselves and so, thank God, we go on living our life. As far as we can, we help the poor and give hospitality to pilgrims. Why, now I have a son who is an officer and a first-rate fellow. And mark this—since the time when I was cured of drunkenness, I have lived under a vow to read the Gospels every single day of my life, one whole Gospel in every twenty-four hours, and I let nothing whatever hinder me. I do this still. If I am exceedingly pressed with business and unusually tired, I lie down and get my wife or my son to read the whole of one of the evangelists to me, and so avoid breaking my rule. By way of thanksgiving and for the glory of God, I have had this book of the Gospels mounted in pure silver, and I always carry it in my breast pocket."

I listened with great joy to this story of his. "I also have come across a case of the same sort," I told him. "At the factory in our village there was a craftsman, very skillful at his job and a good, kindly fellow. Unhappily, however, he also drank, and very often at that. A certain God-fearing man advised him when the desire for drink seized him, to repeat the Prayer of Jesus thirty-three times in honor of the Holy Trinity and in memory of the thirty-three years of the earthly life of Jesus Christ. He took his advice and started to carry it out and, very soon, he quite gave up drinking. And, what is more, three years later he went into a monastery."

"And which is the best," he asked, "the Prayer of Jesus or the Gospels?"

"It's all one and the same thing," I answered. "What the Gospel is, that the Prayer of Jesus is also, for the divine name of Jesus Christ holds in itself the whole gospel truth. The holy Fathers say that the Prayer of Jesus is a summary of the Gospels."

After our talk we said prayers and the major began to read the Gospel of Saint Mark from the beginning, and I listened and said the Prayer in my heart. At two o'clock in the morning he came to the end of the Gospel and we parted and went to bed.

As usual, I got up early in the morning; everyone was still asleep. As soon as it began to get light, I eagerly seized my beloved *Philokalia*. With what gladness I opened it! I might have been getting a glimpse of my own father coming back from a far country, or of a friend risen from the dead. I kissed it and thanked God for giving it back again. I began at once to read Theoleptus of Philadelphia, in the second part of the book. His teaching surprised me when he lays down that one and the same person at one and the same time should do three quite different things. "Seated at table," he says, "supply your body with food, your ear with reading, and your mind with prayer." But the memory of the very happy evening the day before really gave me from my own experience the meaning of this thought. And here also the secret was revealed to me that the mind and the heart are not one and the same thing.

As soon as the major rose, I went to thank him for his kindness and to say good-bye. He gave me tea and a rouble and bade me farewell. I set off again feeling very happy.

I had gone over a half a mile when I remembered I had promised the soldiers a rouble, and that now this rouble had come to me in a quite unlooked-for way. Should I give it to them or not? At first I thought: they beat you and they robbed you; moreover, this money will be of no use to them whatever, since they are under arrest. But afterwards, other thoughts came to me. Remember it is written in the Bible, *"If your enemy hunger, feed him"* and Jesus Christ himself said, *"Love your enemies. If any man will take away your coat let him have your cloak also."* That settled it for me.

I went back and just as I got to the house all the convicts came out to start on the next stage of their march. I went quickly up to my two soldiers; I handed them my rouble and said, "Repent and pray! Jesus Christ loves men. He will not forsake you." And with that I left them and went on my way.

After doing some thirty miles along the main road I thought I would take a bypath so that I might be more by myself and read more quietly. For a long while I walked through the heart of the forest and but rarely came upon a village. At times I passed almost the whole day sitting under the trees and carefully reading *The Philokalia*, from which I gained a surprising amount of knowledge. My heart kindled with desire for union with God by means of interior prayer, and I was eager to learn it under the guidance and control of my book. At the same time, I felt sad that I had no dwelling where I could give myself up quietly to reading all the while.

During this time I read my Bible also, and I felt that I began to understand it more clearly than before, when I had failed to understand many things in it and had often been a prey to doubts. The holy Fathers were right when they said that *The Philokalia* is a key to the mysteries of holy Scripture. With the help it gave me I began to some extent to understand the hidden meaning of the Word of God. I began to see the meaning of such sayings as "The inner secret man of the heart," "true prayer worships in the spirit," "the kingdom is within us," "the intercession of the Holy Spirit with groanings that cannot be uttered," "abide in me," "give me your heart," "to put on Christ," "the betrothal of the Spirit to our hearts," "the cry from the depths of the heart, 'Abba, Father,' " and so on. And when with all this in mind I prayed with my heart, everything around me seemed delightful and marvelous. The trees, the grass, the birds, the earth, the air, the light, seemed to be telling me that they existed for man's sake, that they witnessed to the love of God for man, that everything proved the love of God for man, that all things prayed to God and sang his praise. Thus it was that I came to understand what *The Philokalia* calls "the knowledge of the speech of all creatures," and I saw the means by which conversation could be held with God's creatures.

In this way I wandered about for a long while, coming at length to so lonely a district that for three days I came upon no village at all. My supply of dried bread was used up, and I began to be very much cast down at the thought that I might die of hunger. I began to pray my hardest in the depths of my heart. All my fears went, and I entrusted myself to the will of God. My peace of mind came back to me, and I was in good spirits again.

When I had gone a little further along the road, which here skirted a huge forest, I caught sight of a dog which came out of it and ran along in front of me. I called it, and it came up to me with a great show of friendliness. I was glad and I thought, here is another case of God's goodness! No doubt there is a flock grazing in the forest and this dog belongs to the shepherd. Or perhaps somebody is shooting in the neighborhood. Whichever it is I shall be able to beg a piece of bread if nothing more, for I have eaten nothing for twenty-four hours. Or at least I shall be able to find out where the nearest village is.

After jumping around me for some little time and seeing that I was not going to give him anything, the dog trotted back into the forest along the narrow footpath by which he had come out. I followed, and a few hundred yards further on, looking between the trees, I saw him run into a hole, from which he looked out and began to bark. At the same time, a thin and pale middle-aged peasant came into view from behind a great tree. He asked me where I came from and, for my part, I wanted to know how he came to be there. And so we started a friendly talk.

He took me into his mud hut and told me that he was a forester and that he looked after this particular wood, which had been sold for felling. He set bread and salt before me and we began to talk. "How I envy you," said I, "being able to live so nicely alone in this quiet instead of being like me! I wander from place to place and rub along with all sorts of people."

"You can stop here, too, if you like," he answered. "The old forester's hut is quite near here. It is half ruined but still quite fit to live in in summer. I suppose you have your passport. As far as bread goes, we shall always have plenty of that; it is brought to me every week from my village. This spring here never dries up. For my part, Brother, I have eaten nothing but bread and have drunk nothing but water for the last ten years. This is how things stand. When autumn comes and the peasants have ended their work on the land, some two hundred workmen will be coming to cut down this wood. Then I shall have no further business here, and you will not be allowed to stay either."

As I listened to all this I all but fell at his feet; I felt so pleased. I did not know how to thank God for such goodness. In this unlooked-for way my greatest wish was to be granted me. There were still over four months before next autumn. During all that time I could enjoy the silence and peace needed for a close reading of *The Philokalia* in order to study and learn ceaseless prayer in the heart. So I very gladly stayed there, to live during that time in the hut he showed me.

I talked further with this simple brother who gave me shelter, and he told me about his life and his ideas. "I had quite a good position in the life of our village," said he. "I had a workshop where I dyed cotton and linen, and I lived comfortably enough, though not without sin. I often cheated in business; I was a false swearer; I was abusive; I used to drink and quarrel. In our village there was an old *dyachok*[21] who had a very old book on the Last Judgment. He used to go from house to house and read from it, and he was paid something for doing so. He came to me, too. Give him threepence and a glass of wine into the bargain and he would go on reading all night till the cock crow. There I would sit at my work and listen while he read about the torments that await us in hell. I heard how the living will be changed and the dead raised; how God will come down to judge the world; how the angels will sound the trumpets. I heard of the fire and pitch, and of the worm which will devour sinners.

"One day as I listened, I was seized with horror and I said to myself, what if these torments come upon me? I will set to work to save my soul. It may be that by prayer I can avoid the results of my sins. I thought about this for a long time. Then I gave up my work, sold my house and, as I was alone in the world, I got a place as forester here and all I asked of my *mir*[22] is bread, clothes, and some candles for my prayers. I have been living like this for over ten years now. I eat only once a day and then nothing but bread and water. I get up at cock crow, make my devotions, and say my prayers before the holy icons with seven candles burning. When I make my rounds in the forest during the day, I wear iron chains weighing sixty pounds next my skin. I never grumble, drink neither wine nor beer. I never quarrel with anybody at all, and I have had nothing to do with women and girls all my life.

"At first this sort of life pleased me, but lately other thoughts have come into my mind, and I cannot get away from them. God only knows if I shall be able to pray my sins away in this fashion, and it's a hard life. And is everything written in that book true? How can a dead man rise again? Supposing he has been dead over a hundred years and not even his ashes are left? Who knows if there is really a hell or not? What more is known of a man after he dies and rots? Perhaps the book was written by priests and masters to make us poor fools afraid and keep us quiet. What if we plague ourselves for nothing and give up all our pleasure in vain? Suppose there is no such thing as another life; what then? Isn't it better to enjoy one's earthly life and take it easily and happily? Ideas of this kind often worry me, and I don't know but what I shall not some day go back to my old work."

I heard him with pity. They say, I thought, that it is only the learned and the clever who are free thinkers and believe in nothing! Yet here is one of ourselves, even a simple peasant, a prey to such unbelief. The kingdom of darkness throws open its gates to everyone, it seems, and maybe attacks the simpleminded most easily. Therefore, one must learn wisdom and strengthen oneself with the Word of God as much as possible against the enemy of the soul.

So with the object of helping this brother and doing all I could to strengthen his faith, I took *The Philokalia* out of my knapsack. Turning to chapter 109 of Isaac, I read it to him. I set out to prove to him the uselessness and vanity of avoiding sin merely from fear of the tortures of hell. I told him that the soul could be freed from sinful thoughts only by guarding the mind and cleansing the heart, and that this could be done by interior prayer. I added that, according to the holy Fathers, one who performs saving works simply from the fear of hell follows the way of bondage, and he who does the same just in order to be rewarded with the kingdom of heaven follows the path of a bargainer with God. The one they call a slave, the other a hireling. But God wants us to come to him as sons to their father. He wants us to behave ourselves honorably from love for him and zeal for his service. He wants us to find our happiness in uniting ourselves with him in a saving union of mind and heart.

"However much you spend yourself on treating your body hardly," I said, "you will never find peace of mind that way. And unless you have God in your mind and the ceaseless Prayer of Jesus in your heart, you will always be likely to fall back into sin for the very slightest reason. Set to work upon the ceaseless saying of the Prayer of Jesus. You have such a good chance of doing so here in this lonely place and, shortly, you will see the gain of it. No godless thoughts will then be able to get at you, and the true faith and love for Jesus Christ will be shown to you. You will then understand how the dead will be raised and you will see the Last Judgment in its true light. The Prayer will make you feel such lightness and bliss in your heart that you will be astonished at it yourself, and your wholesome way of life will be neither dull nor troublesome to you."

Then I went on to explain to him as well as I could how to begin, and how to go on ceaselessly with the Prayer of Jesus, and how the Word of God and the writings of the holy Fathers teach us about it. He agreed with it all and seemed to me to be calmer.

Then I left him and shut myself up in the hut which he had shown me. How delighted I was, how calmly happy when I crossed the threshold of that lonely retreat, or rather, that tomb! It seemed to me like a magnificent palace filled with every consolation and delight. With tears of rapture I gave thanks to God and said to myself, here in this peace and quietude I must seriously set to work at my task and beseech God to give me light.

So I started by reading through *The Philokalia* again with great care, from beginning to end. Before long, I had read the whole of it, and I saw how much wisdom, holiness, and depth of insight there was in this book. Still, so many matters were dealt with in it, and it contained such a lot of lessons from the holy Fathers, that I could not very well grasp it all and take in as a single whole what was said about interior prayer. And this was what I chiefly wanted to know, so as to learn from it how to practice ceaseless self-acting prayer in the heart.

This was my great desire, following the divine command in the apostle's words, *"Covet earnestly the best gifts,"* and again, *"Quench not the Spirit."* I thought over the matter for a long time. What was to be done? My mind and my understanding were not equal to the task, and there was no one to explain. I made up my mind to besiege God with prayer. Maybe he would make me understand somehow.

For twenty-four hours I did nothing but pray without stopping for a single moment. At last my thoughts were calmed and I fell asleep. And then I dreamed that I was in my departed *starets'* cell and that he was explaining *The Philokalia* to me. "The holy book is full of profound wisdom," he was saying. "It is a secret treasury of the meaning of the hidden judgments of God. It is not everywhere and to everyone that it is accessible, but it does give to each such guidance as he needs: to the wise, wise guidance; to the simple-minded, simple guidance. That is why you simple folk should not read the chapters one after the other as they are arranged in the book. That order is for those who are instructed in theology. Those who are uninstructed, but who nevertheless desire to learn interior prayer from this book, should take things in this order. (1) First of all read through the book of Nicephorus the monk (in the second part); then, second, read the whole book of Gregory of Sinai, except the short chapters; third, read Simeon the New Theologian on the three forms of prayer and his discourse on faith; and, after that, the book of Callistus and Ignatius. In these Fathers there are full directions and teaching on interior prayer of the heart in a form which everyone can understand.

"And if, in addition, you want to find a very understandable instruction on prayer, turn to the fourth part and find the summarized pattern of prayer by the most holy Callistus, Patriarch of Constantinople."

In my dream I held the book in my hands and began to look for this passage, but I was quite unable to find it. Then he turned over a few pages himself and said, "Here it is. I will mark it for you." He picked up a piece of charcoal from the ground and made a mark in the margin, against the passage he had found. I listened to him with care and tried to fix in my mind everything he said, word for word.

When I woke up it was still dark. I lay still and in thought went over my dream and all that my *starets* had said for me. God knows, thought I, whether it is really the spirit of my departed *starets* that I have seen, or whether it is only the outcome of my own thoughts, because they are so often taken up with *The Philokalia* and my *starets*. With this doubt in my mind I got up, for day was beginning to break, and what did I see? There on the stone which served as a table in my hut lay the book open at the very page which my *starets* had pointed out to me, and in the margin, a charcoal mark just as in my dream! Even the piece of charcoal itself was lying beside the book! I looked in astonishment, for I remembered clearly that the book was not there the evening before, that it had been put, shut, under my pillow and, also, I was quite certain that before there had been nothing where now I saw the charcoal mark.

It was this which made me sure of the truth of my dream and that my revered master of blessed memory was pleasing to God. I set about reading *The Philokalia* in the exact order he had bidden. I read it once, and again a second time, and this reading kindled in my soul a zealous desire to make what I had read a matter of practical experience. I saw clearly what interior prayer means, how it is to be reached, what the fruits of it are, how it filled one's heart and soul with delight, and how one could tell whether that delight came from God, from nature, or from temptation.

So I began by searching out my heart in the way Simeon the

New Theologian teaches. With my eyes shut I gazed in thought, that is, in my imagination, upon my heart. I tried to picture it there in the left side of my breast and to listen carefully to its beating. I started doing this several times a day, for half an hour at a time, and at first I felt nothing but a sense of darkness. But little by little, after a fairly short time, I was able to picture my heart and to note its movement and further, with the help of my breathing, I could put into it and draw from it the Prayer of Jesus in the manner taught by the saints, Gregory of Sinai, Callistus, and Ignatius. When drawing the air in, I looked in spirit into my heart and said, "Lord Jesus Christ," and when breathing out again, I said, "Have mercy on me." I did this at first for an hour at a time, then for two hours, then for as long as I could, and in the end almost all day long. If any difficulty arose, if sloth or doubt came upon me, I hastened to take up *The Philokalia* and read again those parts which dealt with the work of the heart, and then once more I felt ardor and zeal for the Prayer.

When about three weeks had passed, I felt a pain in my heart and then a most delightful warmth, as well as consolation and peace. This aroused me still more and spurred me on more and more to give great care to the sayings of the Prayer so that all my thoughts were taken up with it and I felt a very great joy.

From this time I began to have, from time to time, a number of different feelings in my heart and mind. Sometimes my heart would feel as though it were bubbling with joy, such lightness, freedom, and consolation were in it. Sometimes I felt a burning love for Jesus Christ and for all God's creatures. Sometimes my eyes brimmed over with tears of thankfulness to God, who was so merciful to me, a wretched sinner. Sometimes my understanding, which had been so stupid before, was given so much light that I could easily grasp and dwell upon matters of which, up to now, I had not been able even to think at all. Sometimes that sense of a warm gladness in my heart spread throughout my whole being and I was deeply moved as the fact of the presence of God everywhere was brought home to me. Sometimes, by calling upon the name of Jesus, I was overwhelmed with bliss, and now I knew the meaning of the words *"The kingdom of God is within you."*

From having all these and other like feelings, I noted that interior prayer bears fruit in three ways: in the Spirit, the feelings, and in revelations. In the first, for instance, is the sweetness of the love of God, inward peace, gladness of mind, purity of thought, and the sweet remembrance of God. In the second, the pleasant warmth of the heart, fullness of delight in all one's limbs, the joyous "bubbling" in the heart, lightness and courage, the joy of living, power not to feel sickness and sorrow. And in the last, light given to the mind, understanding of holy Scripture, knowledge of the speech of created things, freedom from fuss and vanity, knowledge of the joy of the inner life and, finally, certainty of the nearness of God and of his love for us.

After spending five months in this lonely life of prayer and such happiness as this, I grew so used to the Prayer that I went on with it all the time. In the end I felt it going on of its own accord within my mind and in the depths of my heart, without any urging on my part. Not only when I was awake but even during sleep, just the same thing went on. Nothing broke into it and it never stopped even for a single moment, whatever I might be doing. My soul was always giving thanks to God and my heart melted away with unceasing happiness.

The time came for the wood to be felled. People began to come along in crowds, and I had to leave my quiet dwelling. I thanked the forester, said some prayers, kissed the bit of the earth which God had deigned to give me, unworthy of his mercy as I was, shouldered my bag of books, and set off.

For a very long while I wandered about in different places until I reached Irkutsk. The self-acting Prayer in my heart was a comfort and consolation all the way; whatever I met with, it never ceased to gladden me, though it did so to different degrees at different times. Wherever I was, whatever I did or gave myself up to, it never hindered things, nor was hindered by them. If I am working at anything, the Prayer goes on by itself in my heart and the work gets on faster. If I am listening carefully to anything or reading, the Prayer never stops. At one and the same time, I am aware of both, just as if I were made into two people or as if there were two souls in my one body. Lord, what a mysterious thing man is! *"How manifold are your works, O Lord! In wisdom you have made them all."*

All sorts of things and many strange adventures happened to me as I went on my way. If I were to start telling them all, I should not end in twenty-four hours. Thus, for example, one winter evening as I was going alone through the forest toward a village which I could see about a mile away, and where I was to spend the night, a great wolf suddenly came in sight and made for me. I had in my hand my *starets'* woolen rosary, which I always carried with me. I struck at the animal with that. Well, the rosary was torn out of my hands and got twisted round the wolf's neck. He leapt away from me, but in jumping through a thorn bush, he got his hind paws caught. The rosary also caught on a bough of a dead tree and he began dashing himself about, but he could not free himself because the rosary was tightening round his throat. I crossed myself in faith and went forward to free him, chiefly because I was afraid that if he tore my rosary away and ran off with it, I should lose my precious rosary. And sure enough, as soon as I got hold of the rosary, the wolf snapped it and fled without leaving a trace. I thanked God, with my blessed *starets* in mind, and I came safe and sound to the village, where I asked for a night's lodging at an inn.

I went into the house. Two men, one of them old and the other middle-aged and heavily built, were sitting at a table in a corner drinking tea. They looked as though they were not just simple folk, and I asked the peasant who was with their horses who they were. He told me that the elder of the two was a teacher at an elementary school, and the other the clerk of the county court. They were both people of the better class. He was driving them to a fair about a dozen miles away. After sitting awhile, I asked the hostess to lend me a needle and thread, came over into the candlelight, and set about mending my broken rosary.

The clerk watched what I was doing and said, "I suppose you have been praying so hard that your rosary broke?"

"It was not I who broke it," I answered, "it was a wolf."

"What! A wolf? Do wolves say their prayers, too?" said he jokingly.

I told them all that had happened and how precious the rosary was to me. The clerk laughed again, saying, "Miracles are always happening with you sham saints! What was there sacred about a thing like that? The simple fact was that you brandished something at the wolf and he was frightened and went off. Of course dogs and wolves take fright at the gesture of throwing, and getting caught on a tree is common enough. That sort of thing very often happens. Where is the miracle?"

But the old man answered him thus: "Do not jump to conclusions like that, sir. You miss the deeper aspects of the incident. For my part, I see in this peasant's story the mystery of nature, both sensuous and spiritual."

"How's that?" asked the clerk.

"Well, like this. Although you have not received the highest education, you have, of course, learned the sacred history of the Old and New Testaments, as summarized in the questions and answers used at school. You remember that when our father Adam was still in a state of holy innocence, all the animals were obedient to him. They approached him in fear and received from him their names. The old man to whom this rosary belonged was a saint. Now what is the meaning of sanctity? For the sinner, it means nothing else than a return through effort and discipline to the state of innocence of the first man. When the soul is made holy the body becomes holy also. The rosary had always been in the hands of a sanctified person; the effect of the contact of his hands and the exhalation of his body was to inoculate it with holy power—the power of the first man's innocence. That is the mystery of spiritual nature! All animals, in natural succession down to the present time, have experienced this power, and they experience it through smelling, for in all animals the nose is the chief organ of sensation. That is the mystery of sensuous nature!"

"You learned people go on about strength and wisdom," said the clerk, "but we take things more simply. Fill up a glass of vodka and tip it off; that will give you strength enough." And he went over to the cupboard.

"That's your business," said the schoolmaster, "but please leave the learning to us."

I liked the way he spoke, and I came up closer to him and said, "May I venture, Father, to tell you a little more about my *starets?*" And so I told him about the appearance of my *starets* while I was asleep, the teaching he had given me, and the charcoal mark which he had made in *The Philokalia.* He listened with care to what I told him, but the clerk, who lay stretched out on a bench, muttered, "It's true enough you can lose your wits through reading the Bible too much. That's what it is! Do you suppose a bogyman comes and marks your books at night? You simply let the book drop on the ground yourself while you were asleep, and some soot made a dirty mark on it. There's your miracle, trickster! I've come across plenty of your kind!"

Muttering this sort of thing, the clerk rolled over with his face to the wall and went to sleep. So I turned to the schoolmaster, saying, "If I may, I will show you the actual book. Look, it is really marked, not just dirtied with soot." I took it out of my knapsack and showed him. "What surprises me," said I, "is how a spirit without a body could have picked up a piece of charcoal and written with it."

He looked at the mark and said, "This also is a spiritual mystery. I will explain it to you. Look here now, when spirits appear in a bodily form to a living person, they create, out of the air and other things, for themselves a body which can be felt, and later on give back to the elements again what they had borrowed from them. Just as the atmosphere possesses elasticity, a power to contract and expand, so the soul, clothed in it, can take up anything and act and write. But what is this book of yours? Let me have a look at it." He began to look at it and it opened at the sermons of Saint Simeon the New Theologian. "Ah, this must be a theological work. I have never seen it before," he said.

"It is almost wholly made up," I told him, "of teaching on interior prayer of the heart in the name of Jesus Christ. It is set forth here in full detail by twenty-five holy Fathers."

"Ah, I know something of interior prayer," he answered.

I bowed before him, down to the very ground, and begged him to speak to me about interior prayer.

"Well, it says in the New Testament that man and all creation *'are subject to vanity, not willingly,'* and sigh with effort and desire to enter into the liberty of the children of God. The mysterious sighing of creation—the innate aspiration of every soul toward God—that is exactly what interior prayer is. There is no need to learn it; it is innate in every one of us!"

"But what is one to do to find it in oneself, to feel it in one's heart, to acknowledge it by one's will, to take it and feel the happiness and light of it, and so to reach salvation?" I asked.

"I don't know whether there is anything on the subject in theological books," said he.

"Well, here it is. It is all explained here," I answered, showing him my book again. The schoolmaster noted the title and said he would certainly have one sent from Tobolsk and study it. After that, we went our different ways. I thanked God for this talk with the schoolmaster, and prayed that God would so order things that the clerk also might read *The Philokalia,* even if only once, and let him find salvation through it.

Another time—it was in spring—I passed through a village where I stayed with a priest. He was a worthy man, living alone, and I spent three days with him. Having watched me for that length of time he said to me, "Stay here. I will pay you something. I need a trustworthy man. As you see, we are starting to build a stone church here near the old wooden chapel, and I have been looking for some honest person to keep an eye on the workmen and stay in the chapel in charge of the offerings for the building fund. It is exactly the thing for you and would just suit your way of life. You will be alone in the chapel and say your prayers. There is a quiet little room for a watchman there. Please stay, at any rate, until the building is finished."

For a long while I refused but, in the end, I had to yield to the good priest's begging, and I stayed there till the autumn, taking up my abode in the chapel. At first I found it quiet and apt for prayer, although a great many people came to the chapel, especially on holidays—some to say their prayers, some because they were bored, and others again with the idea of pilfering from the collection plate. I read my Bible and my *Philokalia* every evening, and some of them saw this and started talking to me about it or asking me to read aloud.

After a while I noticed that a young village girl often came to the chapel and spent a long while in prayer. Listening to her whisperings, I found that the prayers she was saying were strange to me, and others the usual prayers in a garbled form. I asked her where she learned such things, and she told me it was from her mother, who was a church woman, but that her father belonged to a sect which had no priesthood. Feeling sorry for her, I advised her to read her prayers in the right form as given by the tradition of holy Church. Then I taught her the right wording of the Lord's Prayer and of the Hail Mary and, finally, I advised her to say the Prayer of Jesus as often as she could, for that brought one nearer to God than any other prayer. The girl took note of what I said and set about it quite simply. And what happened? A short time afterwards, she told me that she was so used to the Prayer that she felt it draw her all the time, that she used it as much as she could, that she enjoyed the Prayer at the time, and that afterwards she was filled with gladness and a wish to begin using it again. I was glad of this and advised her to go on with it more and more.

Summer was drawing to a close. Many visitors to the chapel came to see me also, not only to be read to and to ask for advice, but with all sorts of worldly troubles—and even to ask about things they had mislaid or lost. Some of them seemed to take me for a wizard. The girl I spoke about also came to me one day in a state of great distress and worry, not knowing what to do. Her father wanted to make her marry a man of his own religion, and they were to be married not by a priest but by a mere peasant belonging to the same sect. "How could that be a lawful marriage? Wouldn't it be the same thing as fornication?" cried the girl. She had made up her mind to run away somewhere or other.

"But," said I, "where to? They would be sure to find you again. They will look everywhere, and you won't be able to hide anywhere from them. You had better pray earnestly to God to turn your father from his purpose and to guard your soul from sin and heresy. That is a much sounder plan than running away."

Thus time passed away, and all this noise and fuss began to be more than I could bear and, at last, at the end of summer, I made up my mind to leave the chapel and go on with my pilgrimage as before. I told the priest what was in my mind, saying, "You know my plans, Father; I must have quiet for prayer, and here it is very disturbing and bad for me, and I have spent the whole summer here. Now let me go and give your blessing on my lonely journey."

But the priest did not want to let me go and tried to get me to stay. "What is there to hinder your praying here? Your work is nothing to speak of, beyond stopping in the chapel. You have your daily bread. Say your prayers then all day and all night if you like, and live with God. You are useful here. You don't go in for silly gossip with the people who come here. You are a source of profit to the church. All that is worth more in God's sight than your prayers all by yourself. Why do you always want to be alone? Common prayer is pleasanter. God did not create man to think of himself only, but that men should help each other and lead each other along the path to salvation, each according to his strength. Think of the saints and the Fathers of the Church! They bustled about day and night; they cared for the needs of the Church; they used to preach all over the place. They didn't sit down alone and hide themselves from people."

"Everyone has his own gift from God," I answered. "There have been many preachers, Father, but there have also been many hermits. Everyone does what he can, as he sees his own line, with the thought that God himself shows him the way of his salvation. How do you get over the fact that many of the saints gave up their positions as bishops or priests or the rule of a monastery and went into the desert to get away from the fuss which comes from living with other people? Saint Isaac the Syrian, for instance, fled from the flock whose bishop he was, and the venerable Athanasius of Athos left his large monastery—just because, to them, these places were a source of temptation and they sincerely believed our Lord's saying, *'What shall it profit a man if he gain the whole world and lose his own soul?'*"

"Ah, but they were saints," said the priest.

"And if," I answered, "the very saints took steps to guard themselves from the dangers of mingling with people, what else, I ask you, can a feeble sinner do?"

So in the end, I said goodbye to this good priest and he, out of the love in his heart, set me on my way.

Some half-dozen miles further on, I stopped for the night at a village. At the inn there I found a peasant hopelessly ill, and I advised those who were with him to see that he had the last sacraments. They agreed and toward morning sent for the parish priest. I stayed there, too, because I wanted to worship and pray in the presence of the Holy Gifts and, going out into the street, sat down on the *zavalina*[23] to wait for the priest to come. All at once, I was astonished to see running toward me from the backyard the girl who used to pray in the chapel.

"What brings you here?" I asked.

"They had fixed the day of my betrothal to the man I told you of, so I left them." And kneeling before me, she went on. "Have pity on me. Take me with you and put me into some convent or other. I don't want to be married. I want to live in a convent and say the Jesus Prayer. They will listen to you and take me."

"Goodness," I exclaimed, "and where am I to take you to? I don't know a single convent in this neighborhood. Besides, I can't take you anywhere without a passport. For one thing, you wouldn't be taken in anywhere and, for another, it would be quite impossible for you to hide nowadays. You would be caught at once and sent home again, and punished as a tramp into the bargain. You had far better go home and say your prayers there. And if you don't want to marry, make out you are ill. The holy mother Clementa did that, and so did the venerable Marina when she took refuge in a men's convent. There are many other cases of the same thing. It is called a saving pretense."

While all this was happening and we sat talking the matter over, we saw four men driving up the road with a pair of horses and coming straight toward us at a gallop. They seized the girl and put her in the cart, and one of them drove off with her. The other three tied my hands together and took me back to the village where I had spent the summer. Their only reply to everything I said for myself was to shout, "We'll teach the little saint to seduce young girls!"

That evening they brought me to the village court, put my feet in irons, and lodged me in jail to await my trial in the morning. The priest heard that I was in prison and came to see me. He brought me some supper and comforted me, saying that he would do what he could for me, and give his word as a spiritual father that I was not the sort of person they thought. After sitting with me for a while, he went away.

The magistrate came late in the evening, driving through the village on his way to somewhere else, and stopped at the deputy's house, where they told him what had happened. He bade the peasants come together, and had me brought to the house which was used as a court. We went in and stood waiting. In comes the magistrate, blustering, and sits down on the table with his hat on.

"Epiphan," he shouts. "Did the girl, this daughter of yours, run off with anything from your house?"

"No, sir, nothing," was the answer.

"Has she been found out doing anything wrong with that fool there?"

"No, sir."

"Well then, this is my decision and my judgment in the matter. You deal with your daughter yourself and, as for this fellow, we will teach him a lesson tomorrow and throw him out of the village with strict orders never to show his face here again. So that's that."

So saying, he got down from the table and went off to bed, while I was taken back to jail. Early in the morning, two country policemen came, flogged me, and drove me out of the village. I went off thanking God that he counted me worthy to suffer for his name. This comforted me and gave still more warmth and glow to my ceaseless interior prayer. None of these things made me feel at all cast down. It was as though they happened to someone else and I merely watched them. Even the flogging was within my power to bear. The Prayer brought sweetness into my heart and made me unaware, so to speak, of everything else.

A mile or two further on, I met the girl's mother coming home from market with what she had bought. Seeing me, she told me that the son-in-law-to-be had withdrawn his suit. "You see, he is annoyed with Akulka for having run away from him." Then she gave me some bread and pastries, and I went on my way.

The weather was fine and dry, and I had no wish to spend the night in a village. So when I came upon two fenced-in haystacks as I went through the forest that evening, I lay down beneath them for a night's lodging. I fell asleep and dreamed that I was walking along and reading a chapter of Saint Anthony the Great from *The Philokalia*. Suddenly, my *starets* overtook me and said, "Don't read that; read this," and pointed to these words in chapter 35 of Saint John Karpathisky: "A teacher submits at times to ignominy and endures pain for the sake of his spiritual children." And again he made me note in chapter 41: "Those who give themselves most earnestly to prayer, it is they who become the prey of terrible and violent temptations." Then he said, "Take courage and do not be downcast. Remember the apostle's words, 'Greater is He that is in you than he that is in the world.' You see that you have now had experience of the truth that no temptation is beyond man's strength to resist and that, with the temptation, God makes also a way of escape. Reliance upon this divine help has strengthened holy men of prayer and led them on to greater zeal and ardor. They not only devoted their own lives to ceaseless prayer but also, out of the love of their hearts, revealed it, and taught it to others as opportunity occurred. Saint Gregory of Thessalonica speaks of this as follows: 'Not only should we ourselves in accordance with God's will pray unceasingly in the name of Jesus Christ, but we are bound to reveal it and teach it to others, to everyone in general, religious and secular, learned and simple, men, women, and children, and to inspire them all with zeal for prayer without ceasing.' In the same way the venerable Callistus Telicudes says, 'One ought not to keep thoughts about God (that is, interior prayer) and what is learned by contemplation and the means of raising the soul on high simply in one's own mind, but one should make notes of it, put it into writing for general use and with a loving motive.' And the Scriptures say in this connection, *'Brother is helped by brother like a strong and lofty city'* (Prov 18:19). Only in this case it is above all things necessary to avoid self praise and to take care that the seed of divine teaching is not sown to the wind."

I woke up feeling great joy in my heart and strength in my soul, and I went on my way. A long while after this, something else happened which also I will tell you about if you like. One day—it was March 24 to be exact—I felt a very urgent wish to make my Communion the next day, that is, on the feast of the Annunciation of our Lady. I asked whether the church was far away and was told it was about twenty miles. So I walked for the rest of that day and all the next night in order to get here in time for matins. The weather was as bad as it could be. It snowed and rained, there was a strong wind, and it was very cold. On my way, I had to cross a small stream and, just as I got to the middle, the ice gave way under my feet and I was plunged into the water up to my waist. Drenched like this, I came to matins and stood through it, and also through the liturgy which followed and at which, by God's grace, I made my Communion.

In order to spend the day quietly and without spoiling my spiritual happiness, I begged the sexton to allow me to stay in his little room until the next morning. I was more happy than I can tell all that day, and my heart was full of joy. I lay on the plank bed in that unheated room as though I were resting on Abraham's bosom. The Prayer was very active. The love of Jesus Christ and of the Mother of God seemed to surge into my heart in waves of sweetness and steep my soul in consolation and triumph.

At nightfall I was seized with violent rheumatic pains in my legs and that brought to my mind that they were soaking wet. I took no notice of it and set my heart the more to my Prayer, so that I no longer felt the pain. In the morning when I wanted to get up I found that I could not move my legs. They were quite paralyzed and as feeble as bits of string. The sexton dragged me down off the bed by main force. And so there I sat for two days without moving. On the third day, the sexton set about turning me out of his room "for," said he, "supposing you die here. What a fuss there will be!"

With the greatest of difficulty, I somehow or other crawled along on my arms and dragged myself to the steps of the church and lay there. And there I stayed like that for a couple of days. The people who went by passed me without taking the slightest notice either of me or of my pleadings. In the end, a peasant came up to me and sat down and talked. And after a while he asked, "What will you give me if I cure you? I had just exactly the same thing once, so I know a medicine for it."

"I have nothing to give you," I answered.

"But what have you got in your bag?"

"Only dried bread and some books."

"Well, what about working for me just for one summer, if I cure you?"

"I can't do any work. As you see, I have only the use of one arm; the other is almost entirely withered."

"Then what can you do?"

"Nothing, beyond the fact that I can read and write."

"Ah! Write! Well, teach my little boy to write. He can read a little, and I want him to be able to write, too. But it costs such a lot; they want twenty roubles to teach him."

I agreed to this, and with the sexton's help he carried me away and put me in an old empty bathhouse in his backyard.

Then he set about curing me. And this was his method. He picked up from the floors, the yards, the cesspools, the best part of a bushel of various sorts of putrid bones, bones of cattle, of birds—all sorts. He washed them, broke them up small with a stone, and put them into a great earthen pot. This he covered with a lid which had a small hole in it, and placed the earthen pot upside down on an empty jar sunk in the ground. He smeared the upper pot with a thick coating of clay and, making a pile of wood round it, he set fire to this and kept it burning for more than twenty-four hours, saying as he fed the fire, "Now we'll get some tar from the bones." Next day, when he took the lower jar out of the ground, there had dripped into it through the hole in the lid of the other jar about a pint of thick, reddish, oily liquid, with a strong smell, like living raw meat. As for the bones left in the jar, from being black and putrid they had become white and clean and transparent like mother of pearl.

I rubbed my legs with this liquid five times a day—and behold, twenty-four hours later I found I could move my toes. Another day, and I could bend my legs and straighten them again. On the fifth day, I stood on my feet and, with the help of a stick, walked about the yard. In a word, in a week's time my legs had become fully as strong as they were before. I thanked God and mused upon the mysterious power which he has given his creatures. Dry, putrid bones, almost brought to dust, yet keeping such vital force, color, smell, power of acting on living bodies and, as it were, giving life to bodies that are half dead! It is a pledge of the future resurrection of the body. How I would like to point this out to that forester with whom I lived, in view of his doubts about the general resurrection!

Having in this way got better from my illness, I began to teach the boy. Instead of the usual copybook work, he wrote out the Prayer of Jesus. I made him copy it, showing him how to set out the words nicely. I found teaching the lad restful, for during the daytime he worked for the steward of an estate nearby and could only come to me while the steward slept, that is, from daybreak till the liturgy.

He was a bright boy and soon began to write fairly well. His employer saw him writing and asked him who had taught him.

"A one-armed pilgrim who lives in our old bathhouse," said the boy.

The steward, who was a Pole, was interested and came to have a look at me. He found me reading *The Philokalia,* and started a talk by asking what I was reading. I showed him the book. "Oh," said he, "that's *The Philokalia.* I've seen the book before at our priest's[24] when I lived at Vilna. They tell me, however, that it contains odd sorts of schemes and tricks for prayer written down by the Greek monks. It's like those fanatics in India and Bokhara who sit down and blow themselves out trying to get a sort of tickling in their hearts and, in their stupidity, take this bodily feeling for prayer and look upon it as the gift of God. All that is necessary to fulfill one's duty to God is to pray simply, to stand and say the Our Father as Christ taught us. That puts you right for the whole day—but not to go on over and over again to the same tune. That, if I may say so, is enough to drive you mad. Besides, it's bad for your heart."

"Don't think in that way about this holy book, sir," I answered. "It was not written by simple Greek monks but by great and very holy men of old time—men whom your Church honors also, such as Anthony the Great, Macarius the Great, Mark the Spiritual Athlete, John Chrysostom, and others. It was from them that the monks of India and Bokhara took over the 'heart method' of interior prayer—only they quite spoiled and garbled it in doing so, as my *starets* explained to me. In *The Philokalia*, all the teaching about the practice of prayer in the heart is taken from the Word of God, from the holy Bible, in which the same Jesus Christ who bade us say the Our Father taught also ceaseless prayer in the heart. For he said, *'You shall love the Lord your God with all your heart and with all your mind,' 'Watch and pray,' 'Abide in Me and I in you.'* And the holy Fathers, calling to witness the holy King David's words in the Psalms, *'O taste and see how gracious the Lord is,'* explain the passage thus: that the Christian ought to use every possible means of seeking and finding delight in prayer, and ceaselessly to look for consolation in it, and not be content with simply saying 'Our Father' once a day. Let me read to you how these saints blame those who do not strive to reach the gladness of the prayer of the heart.

"They write that such do wrong for three reasons. First, because they show themselves against the Scriptures inspired by God and, second, because they do not set before themselves a higher and more perfect state of soul to be reached. They are content with outward virtues only, and cannot hunger and thirst for the truth—and therefore miss the blessedness and joy in the Lord. Third, because, by letting their mind dwell upon themselves and their own outward virtues, they often slip into temptation and pride, and so fall away."

"It is sublime, what you are reading," said the steward, "but it's hardly for us ordinary lay folk, I think!"

"Well, I will read you something simpler, about how people of goodwill, even if living in the world, may learn how to pray without ceasing."

I found the sermon on George the Youth, by Simeon the New Theologian, and read it to him from *The Philokalia*. This pleased him and he said, "Give me that book to read at my leisure, and I will have a good look into it sometime."

"I will let you have it for twenty-four hours with pleasure," I answered, "but not for longer, because I read it every day and I just can't live without it."

"Well then, at least copy out for me what you have just read. I will pay you for your trouble."

"I don't want payment," said I. "I will write that out for you for love's sake and in the hope that God will give you a longing for prayer."

I at once and with pleasure made a copy of the sermon I had read. He read it to his wife and both of them were pleased with it. And so it came about that at times they would send for me and I would go, taking *The Philokalia* with me, and read to them while they sat drinking tea and listening. Once they asked me to stay to dinner. The steward's wife, who was a kindly old lady, was sitting with us at table eating some fried fish, when by some mischance she got a bone lodged in her throat. Nothing we could do gave her any relief and nothing would move the bone. Her throat gave her so much pain that a couple of hours later she had to go and lie down. The doctor (who lived twenty miles away) was sent for and, as by this time it was evening, I went home, feeling very sorry for her.

That night, while I was sleeping lightly, I heard my *starets'* voice. I saw no figure, but I heard him say to me, "The man you are living with cured you. Why then do you not help the steward's wife? God has bidden us feel for our neighbor."

"I would help her gladly," I answered, "but how? I know no means whatever."

"Well, this is what you must do. From her very earliest years she has had a dislike of oil. She not only will not taste it, but cannot bear even the smell of it without being sick. So make her drink a spoonful of oil. It will make her vomit, the bone will come away, the oil will soothe the sore the bone has made in her throat, and she will be well again."

"And how am I to give it her if she dislikes it so? She will refuse to drink it."

"Get the steward to hold her head and pour it suddenly into her mouth, even if you have to use force."

I woke up and went straight off and told the steward all this in detail. "What good can your oil do now?" said he. "She is hoarse and delirious, and her neck is all swollen."

"Well, at any rate, let us try. Even if it doesn't help, oil is at least harmless as a medicine."

He poured some into a wineglass and somehow or other we got her to swallow it. She was violently sick at once and soon vomited up the bone, and some blood with it. She began to feel easier and fell into a deep sleep. In the morning I went to ask after her and found her sitting quietly taking her tea. Both she and her husband were full of wonder at the way she had been cured and, even greater than that, was their surprise that her dislike of oil had been told me in a dream—for apart from themselves, not a soul knew of the fact. Just then the doctor also drove up, and the steward told him what had happened to his wife and I, in my turn, told him how the peasant had cured my legs. The doctor listened to it all and then said, "Neither the one case nor the other is greatly to be wondered at. It is the same natural force which operated in both cases. Still, I shall make a note of it." And he took out a pencil and wrote in his notebook.

After this the report quickly spread through the whole neighborhood that I was a prophet and a doctor and wizard. There began a ceaseless stream of visitors from all parts to bring their affairs and their troubles to my notice. They brought me presents and began to treat me with respect and to look after my comfort. I bore this for a week and then, fearing I should fall into vainglory and harmful distractions, I left the place in secret by night.

Thus once more I set out on my lonely way, feeling as light as if a great weight had been taken off my shoulders. The Prayer comforted me more and more so that at times my heart bubbled over with boundless love for Jesus Christ and, from my delight in this, streams of consolation seemed to flow through my whole being. The remembrance of Jesus Christ was so stamped upon my mind that as I dwelt upon the Gospel story, I seemed to see its events before my very eyes. I was moved even to tears of joy and sometimes felt such gladness in my heart that I am at a loss even how to tell of it.

It happened at times that for three days together I came upon no human dwelling and, in the uplifting of my spirit, I felt as though I were alone on the earth, one wretched sinner before the merciful and loving God. This sense of being alone was a comfort to me and it made me feel my delight in prayer much more than when I was mixing with a crowd of people.

At length I reached Irkutsk. When I had prayed before the relics of Saint Innocent, I began to wonder where I should go now. I did not want to stay there for a long while; it was a town in which many people lived. I was walking thoughtfully along the street when I came upon a certain merchant belonging to the place. He stopped me saying, "Are you a pilgrim? Why not come home with me?" We went off together and he took me into his richly furnished house and asked me about myself. I told him all about my travels and then he said, "You ought to go on a pilgrimage to Jerusalem. There are shrines there the like of which are not to be found anywhere else!"

"I should be only too glad to do so," I answered, "but I haven't the money. I can get along on dry land till I come to the sea, but I have no means of paying for a sea voyage, and it takes a good deal of money."

"How would you like me to find the money for you? I have already sent one of our townsfolk there, an old man, last year," said the merchant.

I fell at his feet and he went on to say, "Listen, I will give you a letter to my son at Odessa. He lives there and has business connections with Constantinople. He will be pleased to give you a passage on one of the vessels to Constantinople, and to tell his agents there to book a passage to Jerusalem for you on another boat, and pay for it. That is not so very expensive."

I was overcome with joy when I heard this and thanked my benefactor for his kindness. Even more did I thank God for showing me such fatherly love, and for his care for me, a wretched sinner who did no good either to himself or to anyone else, and ate the bread of others in idleness. I stayed three days with this kindly merchant. As he had promised, he wrote me a letter to his son, so here I am now on my way to Odessa, planning to go on till I reach Jerusalem. But I do not know whether the Lord will allow me to venerate his life-giving tomb.

Commentary II

Prayer of the Heart

*There came into my heart a gracious warmth which spread
through my whole breast.*

FROM *THE WAY OF A PILGRIM*

෧

T he second narrative follows the author on a pilgrimage to the
city of Irkutsk, in Siberia, to visit the tomb of Saint Innocent. On the way there, he interrupts his journey twice: to spend
five months deep in the Siberian forest in the solitude of a deserted
mud hut, and to work the summer months of the following year as a
watchman for the priest of a small village as he constructs a new
chapel for his community. The narrative relates the Pilgrim's journey to the mud hut, his time in the hut, his departure from the hut
and journey to the chapel, his time watching the chapel, and his
departure from the chapel and final journey to Irkutsk. When examined with care, each of these episodes reveals something important
about the prayer of the heart and the nature of the spiritual-direction
relationship.

THE PILGRIM'S JOURNEY TO THE MUD HUT

Summary
With the death of the *starets*, the Pilgrim desires to settle down and immerse himself in *The Philokalia*. A childhood disability in his left hand, however, prevents him from managing the upkeep of a permanent residence. With no place to turn to, he resumes his life of wandering, this time by setting out on a holy pilgrimage to the provincial city of Irkutsk.

On the road, he reads from this holy book whenever he can. Sometimes he spends the entire day sitting in the forest immersing himself in it. So moved is he by what he finds there that he decides to do most of his traveling by night so as to have more daylight hours for studying it. For more than two months, he lives in this simple and carefree manner. Whenever he comes to a village, he asks for a handful of salt and some dry bread, fills his jar with water, and sets out on his way for another seventy miles or so.

It is during this time of carefree wandering that the Pilgrim begins to experience what his *starets* had told him about the prayer of the heart. He describes his deep longing for solitude and his desire to immerse himself in the study of *The Philokalia* in order "to go more and more deeply into it and, with faith and heartfelt prayer, to learn from it teaching about the truth for the salvation of my soul."[25]

He begins his journey to Irkutsk, repeating the Jesus Prayer continually on his lips. He has been so well trained by his *starets* in this outward structure that, within a short time, he feels the prayer moving of its own accord from his lips into his heart. At this point, he stops reciting the words of the Prayer completely and begins to listen attentively to the words of his heart in rhythm with its natural beating: "*one*, 'Lord,' *two*, 'Jesus,' *three*, 'Christ,' and so on."[26]

The Pilgrim also begins to experience a delicate soreness in his heart and is so filled with a deep love for Jesus that he seems almost to see him. This warmth in the Pilgrim's heart moves him to delve even deeper into *The Philokalia*. He does this both to verify what he has experienced and to further his studies in the meaning and practice of interior prayer. He wants to make sure that he is not deluding himself and that he is well versed in the teaching of the holy Fathers.

The Pilgrim is truly awed by the wisdom revealed to him through *The Philokalia*. He sees it as the key to understanding not only the Bible but also the language of creation. What he does not understand is clarified by the effects of this interior prayer of the heart. At times, his *starets* would visit him in his dreams and explain things even further. The prayer of the heart protects the Pilgrim from the ravages of despair and enables him to lift to God all of the circumstances of his life. Through it, he is able to give himself entirely over to God and is filled with joy and peace.

That is not to say that the Pilgrim does not encounter trouble along the way. At the end of the summer, two renegade soldiers beat him up and steal his knapsack, his Bible, and his copy of *The Philokalia*. The Pilgrim, understandably, is downcast and weeps bitterly, not so much at the pain but at the loss of his books. He learns in a dream about his *starets*, however, that the incident is a lesson for him on detachment from material things.

The Pilgrim is strengthened by this insight and eventually recovers his books and knapsack when he finds the two soldiers in a group of prisoners under military escort and befriends their commanding officer. In recovering these items, he learns of the officer's own love and devotion for the Bible and hears his story of how, with its aid, he was able to overcome a severe drinking problem. The Pilgrim rejoices in the officer's account of his conversion and shares with him his own love for what the holy Fathers refer to as "a summary of the Gospels," that is, the Jesus Prayer.[27]

Reflection

The Pilgrim's experiences on this leg of his journey provide a number of helpful insights into both the nature of the prayer of the heart and the dynamics of the relationship of spiritual guidance. In the first place, it is important to note that once the prayer of the lips has become an ingrained habit of the Pilgrim's daily existence, it descends of its own accord ("by itself") into his heart. The Prayer moves from the lips to the mind and then descends into the heart. This anthropological descent is aided by the Pilgrim's deep desire for solitude and the hours upon hours he spends in the study of the sayings of the holy Fathers in *The Philokalia*.

The habit of repetitive vocal prayer, solitude, and study are the conditions that allow the interior prayer of the heart to develop and take root in the Pilgrim's soul. Once the Prayer moves to his heart, the Pilgrim's attitude becomes one of attentive listening to the words as they rise up within him in constant harmony with the beating of his heart. The effects of this interior form of prayer are physical, mental, and spiritual. His soreness of heart, the clarity it brings to his reading of the Scriptures and his understanding of creation, and his longing for an even deeper solitude reveal something of the slow, gradual transformation that is taking place in him. This conversion of life is most manifest in the way he is able to find the hand of God even in the most trying and difficult of circumstances, and in his desire to share with others the fruits of his spiritual journey.

As far as spiritual guidance is concerned, it is clear on this stage of his journey that *The Philokalia* is increasingly becoming the Pilgrim's primary external spiritual resource. He reads it with eager attention whenever he has the chance. This desire for holy reading, in fact, is what moves him to make his pilgrimage through the dismal forest areas of Siberia to the tomb of Bishop Innocent in the provincial city of Irkutsk. Traversing such a lonely landscape, he thinks, would be more conducive to prayer and study.

Even more interesting is the bond that the Pilgrim's holy reading creates with his recently departed *starets*. The spiritual teaching of *The Philokalia* is the link that binds both teacher and pupil, even beyond the pale of death. The more the Pilgrim immerses himself in the teachings of this holy book, the more he embodies the spirit and teaching of the *starets* himself, a man who was totally enamored of the book and the holy Fathers it represents. The appearance of the *starets* in the Pilgrim's dreams is a sign of their close spiritual union that will deepen as the Pilgrim grows in his knowledge of the sacred mysteries contained in the holy book.

By immersing himself in the sayings of *The Philokalia,* the Pilgrim also becomes more and more a part of that holy community of teachers who fill its pages. Careful to scrutinize all of his experience in light of their teachings, he delves deeper into the insights its pages afford. Through the tradition of this living community of faith, the Pilgrim's insights into the Scripture, the language of creation, indeed, the very meaning of life, give birth to and then nourish a rich interior life of faith.

THE PILGRIM'S TIME IN THE HUT

Summary

As the Pilgrim slowly makes his way through Siberia, he comes upon a stray dog who leads him to a thin and pale middle-aged peasant. As he and the peasant partake of a scant meal of bread and water, the Pilgrim learns that there is another mud hut, not far from the place where they are sitting, that would be an ideal place for him to live in solitude and immerse himself ever more deeply in the teachings of *The Philokalia.* The Pilgrim jumps at this possibility and looks forward to spending some time in solitude in the middle of this lonely Siberian forest. He is told that he will not have to leave until the late fall when the trees in that section of the forest will be felled.

The Pilgrim's experiences in this part of his journey number among the most profound of his entire life. As he gets to know the peasant forester and listens to his story, he gradually realizes that, for all his simple living and austere practices, the poor man is beset with doubts that touch the core of the Christian faith, most especially belief in the Resurrection and the Last Judgment. The Pilgrim, thinking that such doubts are normally entertained by more educated people, is amazed that they can take root in the heart of a simple peasant.

Moved by an intense desire to share his own good fortune with this poor, wavering forester, the Pilgrim opens *The Philokalia* and begins to share with him the secrets of the Jesus Prayer. He reminds the forester that, in and of themselves, ascetical practices get a people nowhere if they do not keep the remembrance of God in mind. Citing chapter 109 of Isaac, he explains to him "that soul could be freed from sinful thoughts only by guarding the mind and cleansing the heart, and that this could be done by interior prayer."[28] The Pilgrim promises the forester that, with the practice of the Jesus Prayer, he will see the benefits in no time: godless thoughts will leave him; he will acquire faith and love for Jesus; and he will see the truth of the doctrines of the Resurrection and the Last Judgment. The forester shows interest in the Pilgrim's words and receives instruction in the rudiments of the Jesus Prayer. Once this is done, the Pilgrim feels free to leave the peasant and to take up his lodging in a small mud hut in another part of the forest.

To the Pilgrim, this simple mud hut seems like a magnificent palace. He is filled with thanks to God for the good fortune of being able to pray and study in the midst of such solitude. He opens *The Philokalia* with the intention of reading it from beginning to end, but soon discovers that it is filled with so many different teachings of the holy Fathers that he is unable to learn all that he really wants to know about interior prayer. After thinking for a long time about what to do, he decides to batter the Lord with prayers for enlightenment. He does so for the next twenty-four hours without stopping. That night, his thoughts are calm as he falls into a deep sleep and dreams that he is sitting in the cell of his departed *starets*. There, the *starets* informs the Pilgrim that *The Philokalia* contains something for both the wise and the simpleminded. The latter, the *starets* tells the Pilgrim, should not attempt to read it from beginning to end but, rather, in a simple order that focuses on the interior prayer of the heart:

(1) First of all read through the book of Nicephorus the monk (in part 2); then (2) the whole book of Gregory of Sinai, except the short chapters; (3) Simeon the New Theologian on the three forms of prayer and his discourse on faith; and after that (4) the book of Callistus and Ignatius.[30]

The *starets* goes on to tell him that "[i]n these Fathers there are full directions and teaching on interior prayer of the heart in a form which everyone can understand."[31] For an even clearer teaching on prayer, he suggests that the Pilgrim turn to section 4 for the summary on methods of prayer by the most holy Callistus, Patriarch of Constantinople. The *starets* marks this last passage in *The Philokalia* with a piece of charcoal. Much to his surprise, the Pilgrim awakes to find his own copy of *The Philokalia* opened to that very passage and with the very markings of charcoal exactly as he had dreamed it the night before.

That day, the Pilgrim reads through all the material—twice—in the order that the *starets* had revealed. He finds himself burning with a desire to experience personally all that he has read: the means for attaining interior prayer, its fruits, the delights of soul and heart, and how to discern if it is from God, natural causes, or delusion. He is particularly taken by the simple instructions of Saint Simeon the New Theologian, who tells his disciples to close their eyes and gaze mentally into the heart to try to visualize the heart in the left part of the chest and to listen carefully to its breathing; to do this one half hour several times a day; to repeat the Jesus Prayer in steady rhythm with their breathing; and, when they grow tired of this, to turn immediately to reading *The Philokalia*. He also follows the instructions of Saint Gregory of Sinai, Callistus, and Ignatius with regard to praying the Jesus Prayer in conjunction with the rhythm of his breathing, inhaling with the words "Lord Jesus Christ" and exhaling with "have mercy on me."

At first, he does this exercise for only an hour or two at a time, but eventually is able to do it throughout the entire day. Whenever he gets tired, he turns immediately to *The Philokalia*, and reads specifically those passages dealing with the prayer of the heart.

The Pilgrim experiences many things as a result of these exercises of interior prayer of the heart, beginning with a soreness in the heart that is followed by a most delightful kind of warmth, joy, and peace. Sometimes he feels totally enraptured and filled with a deep and burning love of Jesus. All in all, he notices three major effects of the prayer of the heart: (1) those in the spirit, (2) those in the feelings, and (3) those pertaining to revelations. He describes them in this way:

> In the first...is the sweetness of the love of God, inward peace, gladness of mind, purity of thought, and the sweet remembrance of God. In the second, the pleasant warmth of the heart, fullness of delight in all one's limbs, the joyous "bubbling" in the heart, lightness and courage, the joy of living, power not to feel sickness and sorrow. And in the last, light given to the mind, understanding of holy Scripture, knowledge of the speech of created things, freedom from fuss and vanity, knowledge of the joy of the inner life and, finally, certainty of the nearness of God and of his love for us.[32]

The pilgrim practices the prayer of the heart continuously and experiences all of these effects in his life. It gets to the point that his mind and his heart can recite the Prayer without any effort on his part and he continues without interruption, even when he is sleeping. It is at this stage of his journey, in a small mud hut deep in the forest of Siberia, when he reaches the heights of the interior prayer of the heart.

Reflection
On this leg of his journey, the Pilgrim receives his clearest teaching yet on the practice and effects of the interior prayer of the heart.

True to form, the narrative also provides some valuable information on the dynamics of spiritual direction.

First, the Pilgrim finds himself in a situation in which he himself is called on to offer spiritual guidance. He does this even while he himself is still in the process of learning about the practice of unceasing interior prayer. This tells us that what we receive by way of spiritual nourishment must also be shared with those in need. The Pilgrim views what he finds in *The Philokalia* as something to be shared with others: for their benefit, to be sure, but also for his own. It is interesting to note that his *starets* visits him in his dreams only after he has reached out and offered to another what little bit he has learned about unceasing prayer. The event also tells us that spiritual directors need ongoing guidance and direction for themselves. The Pilgrim is able to help the forester only because he himself has grappled with and made his way through many of the same difficulties.

Second, the narrative underscores the importance of presenting a spiritual classic (such as *The Philokalia*) in a way that is practical and easily digestible for the ordinary reader. Traditions of spiritual guidance that look to such spiritual classics must be sensitive to the situation of the readers and be ready to show them how to read the material and what to look for. If this is not done, readers may find themselves overwhelmed. Directors who suggest books for their directees should make every effort to recommend material that addresses their directees where they are. That is not to say that books of deep spiritual substance must be watered down, only that they need to be adapted, or at least explained, in much the same way that the *starets* explains *The Philokalia* to the Pilgrim. This is often best done in a spiritual reading group that focuses on a particular spiritual classic and discusses it at length under the guidance of an expert.

Finally, the narrative makes it clear that the relationship of direction between the *starets* and the Pilgrim is so deep that it continues even beyond death. The *starets* makes a deep impression on the

Pilgrim, so much so that he lives on in the Pilgrim's unconscious and guides him in and through his dreams. Spiritual directors must seek to develop a close relationship of trust with their directees, guiding them in such a way that the questions they ask will be internalized and remembered long after the relationship of direction has come to an end. This is another way of helping the directee to become self-directed. In this respect, the visit of the *starets* in the Pilgrim's dream can be interpreted as a sign that the latter is internalizing his spiritual father's teaching and will seek to carry it out in his waking hours.

THE PILGRIM'S DEPARTURE FROM THE HUT AND JOURNEY TO THE CHAPEL

Summary

After five months, it is time for the felling of the trees in the area, and the Pilgrim decides to leave his place of solitude and continue his journey to Irkutsk. This section of the narrative is a transitional piece intended to link the Pilgrim's experiences in the hut with those of the chapel in Irkutsk—the two most memorable periods of the second narrative, both of which are united by virtue of the fact that the Pilgrim stays put and is not traveling on the road. Between these periods, he has many wonderful experiences, so many in fact, that an entire day would not be enough to recount them all. What he does offer us is an account of how he was saved by his prayer rope (rosary) from the jaws of a hungry wolf, and a general summary of his experience of the interior prayer of the heart "on the road." The value of this transitional part of the second narrative is to remind us of the universal quality of the prayer of the heart, that is, how it functions in all circumstances of our lives, not just those of solitude.

After packing his things and starting out again in the direction of Irkutsk, the Pilgrim recounts how, early one winter evening, he is attacked by a wolf and manages to escape with his life only when the prayer rope, dangling around the hungry beast's throat, causes the wolf to somehow get entangled in a thorny bush. Later, a sympathetic teacher and a skeptical clerk discuss this miraculous deliverance with the Pilgrim, showing how widely different interpretations can be given to the same set of circumstances.

For his part, the Pilgrim has no doubts whatsoever about the meaning of his deliverance: God has saved him. The self-acting prayer of the heart has been his consolation and joy in this and other experiences. He is able to find the hand of God in whatever happens to him; God is always with him. Whether he is at work, attentively listening to someone, or reading from the holy books, his heart continues to pray without ceasing. The Prayer even *helps* him in what he is doing. Because of it, he works faster, listens more attentively, and reads with greater comprehension. He is simultaneously aware of whatever activity he happens to be engaged in *and* the Prayer that is constantly rising within his heart. It is almost as if he has been divided in two, or as if there are two souls in his one body. He praises God for the mystery of the human person and utters the words of the psalmist: "How manifold are your works, O Lord! In wisdom you have made them all."[33]

Reflection

In many ways, this transitional part of the narrative reveals more about the interior prayer of the heart than all the others combined. So deeply intertwined has it become with the Pilgrim's life that it rises up within his heart without any effort at all. So much has it become a part of his daily activities that it is hardly distinguishable from the other actions of his day. He marvels that he is able to pray in this way, while carrying on all the other activities of his life.

In this transitional section, we see the end result of all that the *starets*, *The Philokalia*, and the Bible have done in the Pilgrim's life. They have become completely internalized and, along with them, the unceasing interior prayer of the heart made possible by the Jesus Prayer. With the name of Jesus now firmly rooted in his heart, everything else in the Pilgrim's life seems easier to deal with. Even the attack of a hungry wolf and the verbal barbs of an unbelieving clerk do not seem to phase him. It is for this reason that the words of the psalmist spring so easily to his lips.

As far as spiritual direction is concerned, this part of the narrative reminds us that, more often than not, the most significant part of direction occurs not during the actual sessions themselves, but outside them, "on the journey" so to speak, when we are called to live out our innermost beliefs in the day-to-day experiences of life. It also reminds us that God's action in our life is usually a question of recognizing the divine hand in ordinary and, at times, difficult tasks. Just as the Pilgrim finds renewed vigor in his work, his listening, and his reading, so too can directees experience the presence of God in the humblest and most mundane of their daily activities.

THE PILGRIM'S TIME AS WATCHMAN OF THE CHAPEL

Summary

In the springtime, the Pilgrim comes to a village where he finds lodging for the night at a priest's house. While there, he receives an offer to stand watch in an old wooden chapel as a new stone chapel is built beside it. He tries to get out of doing this, but finally gives in to the priest's plea for help.

At first, the Pilgrim finds the chapel environment conducive to prayer, even though it is constantly filled with visitors—some who come to pray, others to dawdle, and still others to steal from the collection plate. He reads the Bible and *The Philokalia* regularly to those who are interested and, eventually, gains a reputation as a counselor and sage. In the process, he is able to help a great number of people.

The Pilgrim notices, for example, a young peasant girl who comes frequently to the chapel. She spends a long time in prayer, uttering a number of odd-sounding prayers. As it turns out, the girl's father is a member of a schismatic sect that denies the holy priesthood. Moved with pity, the Pilgrim suggests to the girl that she make a habit of reciting the Jesus Prayer. She takes his advice, receives instructions and, after a short period of time, finds that she has become so accustomed to saying it that she feels as though she is praying it continuously. As a result, she is filled with joy, gladness, and a deep desire to pray without ceasing.

The Pilgrim helps many such visitors in this and similar ways. As time goes on, however, he finds the small wooden chapel becoming too noisy and full of distractions for his own peace of mind. He goes to the village priest and tells him of his desire to leave. What ensues is a rather long debate between the Pilgrim and the priest about the tension between action and contemplation, with the priest taking the side of action ("Why do you always want to be alone?") and the Pilgrim taking the side of contemplation ("Everyone has his own gift from God").[34] Finally, at the end of the summer, the Pilgrim parts with the priest on amicable terms. As he leaves the village, however, he is ridiculed, beaten, and jailed for a crime he never committed. He gains his release only after the village priest intercedes for him and he promises never again to return to the village.

Reflection

This leg of the Pilgrim's journey shows the extent to which those deeply immersed in the interior prayer of the heart can involve themselves in a life of action. For the Pilgrim, the small chapel turns out to be a busy center of apostolic witness. He finds himself dealing with lots of people—people who have come there for all sorts of reasons and who live on different spiritual levels. The reputation he has earned as an advisor points to his ability to meet the people where they are and to help them deal with their very practical problems. Such wisdom comes not from his own abilities but from the power of unceasing prayer, which guides him in the Spirit and helps him, moment by moment, in even the most mundane affairs.

In all this activity, however, the Pilgrim eventually reaches his limit. Tired and worn out by noise and countless distractions, he desires to stop what he is doing and look for a quieter place where he can pray in solitude and commune with God. Before he can do that, however, he suffers both physical and psychological harm from those who misunderstand his deeds and intentions.

This episode highlights the tension between action and contemplation that exists in nearly every understanding of the spiritual life. It also demonstrates how, to a large extent, the prayer of the heart helps create a harmonious balance between the two by relegating them to different anthropological dimensions of human living. We should remember, however, that the Pilgrim himself needs to undergo a long and arduous journey in order to arrive at the interior prayer of the heart. It would be a mistake to think that the balance between action and contemplation can be arrived at overnight or with only a modicum of effort. The fact that even the Pilgrim reaches a point when he needs to escape the hustle and bustle of the small wooden chapel shows how precarious a balance it really is— one that must be constantly examined and checked in light of the particular circumstances of our own individual lives.

The Pilgrim's journey to the mud hut, and then from the mud hut to the small wooden chapel, points to the similar journey each person must make first into solitude, and then from solitude to a life of action. That journey is made not once, but many times in a person's life—indeed many times each day.

Spiritual directors should help directees discern their own balance between action and contemplation, helping them realize that the two do not exist in isolation from each other but, in fact, complement each other and actually need each other. As we have already seen many times in the narrative, the prayer of the heart inserts itself naturally into a life of action. What is less evident in the text, but which we well understand probably all too well, is the way a life of action, when cut off from its roots in prayer and solitude, can so easily dry up and wither. It is essential that people who, like the Pilgrim, are helping others find their way to God be keenly attuned to maintaining an appropriate balance between action and contemplation in their own lives. In the same way, when a spiritual director loses that balance, the damage done to others is often great.

DEPARTURE FROM THE CHAPEL AND ARRIVAL IN IRKUTSK

Summary

After leaving the village, the Pilgrim continues his way through the forest to the provincial city of Irkutsk. Late that evening he comes across two haystacks and decides to bed down there for the night.

In his dreams, the Pilgrim sees himself walking along the road and reading from the works of Saint Anthony the Great in *The Philokalia.* Suddenly his *starets* catches up with him, tells him he is reading the wrong passage, and directs him, instead, to the thirty-fifth and forty-first chapters of Saint John Karpathisky. Respectively, these chapters deal with the suffering a teacher must sometimes undergo for the spiritual benefit of others, and the terrible and fierce temptations that assail those who pray with the greatest intensity. Quoting 1 John 4:4 and 1 Corinthians 10:13, the *starets* then gives the Pilgrim some of his own advice: "Take courage and do not be downcast." He goes on to say that "[r]eliance upon divine help has strengthened holy men of prayer and led them on to greater zeal and ardor."[35] He also reminds the Pilgrim that those who gave their lives over to unceasing prayer also revealed and taught it to others whenever opportunities presented themselves. He cites passages from Saint Gregory of Thessalonica, the venerable Callistus Telicudes, and the holy Bible (Prov 18:19) to back up his claims. The *starets* goes on to tell the Pilgrim that a person must flee vanity and be always on guard, lest God's Word is sown in the wind.

When the Pilgrim awakes, his heart is filled with joy and his soul is strengthened. As he goes on his way he is comforted by his prayers and is deeply moved, physically, mentally, and emotionally, by the remembrance of Jesus Christ. So deep is this experience of being in the presence of the Lord that when he meditates on the biblical events, he feels as though he could see them happening right before his eyes. In his solitude, the Pilgrim travels great distances accompanied only by the interior prayer of his heart. He senses that solitude enables him to experience the delights of this prayer with far greater sensitivity than when he is with other people.

During this stage of his journey, the Pilgrim walks the better part of a day and a night in order to arrive at a church and receive the holy Eucharist on the feast of the Annunciation. The weather is harsh and his legs become stiff and numb from the cold, especially when he falls through the ice of a stream. In repayment for treatment and cure, he agrees to teach a peasant's son how to read and even manages to cure a woman of a throat ailment. As a result, the Pilgrim gains a reputation throughout the district as a prophet, doctor, and wizard. Troubled by his newfound fame and afraid that distraction and vainglory will ruin his spiritual life, he decides to leave the district in secret under the cover of darkness.

When he finally arrives in Irkutsk, he venerates the relics of Bishop Innocent and then begins to wonder what he should do next. He meets a local merchant who convinces him to make a pilgrimage to Jerusalem. The merchant even offers to write a letter of introduction to his son in Odessa who, in turn, will gladly arrange passage for the Pilgrim, first from Odessa to Constantinople by sea, and then from Constantinople to Jerusalem—all at his own expense. Upon hearing these remarks, the Pilgrim is overcome with joy and resolves to take up the merchant's generous offer.

Reflection
On this last leg of his journey to Irkutsk, the Pilgrim learns an important lesson from his *starets* about the nature of the interior prayer

of the heart. Tired and worn out by his previous apostolic activity in the small wooden chapel, the Pilgrim is encouraged by his *starets* to be strong and not to lose hope when it comes to sharing with others what he has learned about the prayer of the heart. Those who practice this prayer are called to share it with others; they are moved instinctively to share it with anyone who might benefit from its fruits (for example, "to everyone in general, religious and secular, learned and simple, men, women, and children"[36]). The *starets* guides the Pilgrim through select passages of the Bible and *The Philokalia* that show how the fruits of contemplation ultimately manifest themselves in action. He teaches the Pilgrim this difficult lesson because he is ready for it. Experience has already shown the Pilgrim how difficult it can be to maintain one's composure in the midst of strenuous apostolic activity as well as undeserved suffering.

The Pilgrim comes to recognize that, although it is much easier for him to experience the delights of interior prayer in solitude, part of his calling is to help others learn the secrets of the Jesus Prayer. One might say that the Pilgrim receives a deeper insight into the nature of his calling. He who has been slowly and patiently taught by his *starets*—both in life and in death—the meaning and the practice of interior prayer must carry on the tradition and do the same for others. In time he will find that it makes no difference whatsoever whether he is living in solitude or in the midst of many people—the unceasing prayer of the heart will be as intense as ever. Understandably, after dreaming of his *starets* in this way, the Pilgrim experiences an intense desire to receive the holy Eucharist, the sacrament *par excellence* of communion with Christ's Mystical Body.

At the end of his journey, when he finally arrives at Irkutsk, the Pilgrim, surprisingly, spends hardly any time on the relics of Saint Innocent—his reason for coming to Irkutsk in the first place. In a single phrase he mentions that he venerated the holy relics and then, in the very next phrase, he wonders what he should do next. The matter-of-fact way in which he deals with arriving at the goal of his journey tells us that it is not so much the destination but the journey itself that is important for the prayer of unceasing and, hence, for the entire spiritual life. That the Pilgrim decides at this very point to embark on a pilgrimage to the holy city of Jerusalem indicates that a person's spiritual journey is unending and always involves an invitation—presented symbolically by the generous merchant—to delve more and more deeply into the mystery of Christ.

As far as spiritual direction is concerned, this last section of the second narrative should alert directors of the importance of knowing when to challenge and when to console their directees. The Pilgrim leaves the small wooden chapel tired, worn out, uncertain about his ability to pray without ceasing in the midst of so many people, and distressed by the mistreatment he receives from the hands of others. The *starets* encourages him and tells him not to lose heart. At the same time, he challenges the Pilgrim with the words of the holy Fathers, who insist that such a harmony is not only possible, but actually represents the height of the interior prayer of the heart. In a similar way, directors should help their directees step-by-step through the long, arduous process of living a life of contemplation in a world of action.

On another level, the fact that the Pilgrim is ready to begin another, even more demanding, pilgrimage almost immediately upon finishing the one to the relics of Bishop Innocent of Irkutsk indicates the never-ending nature of our spiritual journeys and the importance of not being complacent in our present place along the way. It is easy for us to get so attached to a particular kind of spirituality that the expression of it eventually becomes more important than our relationship with God.

At the end of the second narrative, the Pilgrim is ready to move on just as soon as he arrives at his goal. This requires of him a certain openness to responding to the inspirations of the Spirit that come to him in the concrete circumstances of the day and a willingness to see to and respond to the hand of Providence in the present moment. Directors should encourage their directees to respond to the movements of God's hand in their lives in a similar way.

CONCLUSION

In this second narrative, the author completes two journeys: one to the holy relics of Saint Innocent of Irkutsk, the other into the depths of his heart. One is outward, the other is inward. One requires dried bread and water for survival; the other feeds on the unceasing interior prayer of the heart. At this point of the author's tale, the way of the Pilgrim and the way of the mystic have become deeply and inextricably intertwined, so much so that one cannot be separated from the other without doing grave damage to each.

In one sense, the Pilgrim's story ends here with his arrival in Irkutsk. Although he states his intention of setting out on pilgrimage to Jerusalem, and demonstrates every intention of getting there, we never find out if he accomplishes his task. We see this in the fact that the third and fourth narratives of the book do not follow the Pilgrim on his subsequent journeys but comprise, instead, a series of autobiographical reflections on his early life and experiences as a pilgrim prior to his most recent journey to Irkutsk. Such reflection, coming as it does midway through the book, brings to the fore the importance of reflection for the Pilgrim's (as well as our own) spiritual well-being. Without it, the journey to Jerusalem cannot take place and he will never reach his final goal.

In this second narrative, the Pilgrim covers a great deal of ground—both physically and spiritually. He wanders through the lonely forests of Siberia and journeys though the desolate regions of his soul. All during this time, he takes to heart all that he has learned from the Bible, *The Philokalia*, and his recently departed *starets,* and allows them to become an integral part of himself. In doing so, his journey is one toward spiritual maturity. His responsibilities are now immense: what he has received he now must impart; what he himself owns he must now offer to others. He himself will be asked to be a *starets* for others, and he has already learned something of what this entails. At the symbolic age of thirty-three he will have the rest of his life, however long that may be, to guide others along the interior paths of the heart.

REFLECTION QUESTIONS

1. The Pilgrim has a withered left hand. What physical, psychological, and spiritual wounds do you bear and are destined to carry through life? Are you embarrassed by them? How do they hinder you from becoming the type of person you wish to be? Have they in any way helped you in your relationships with others? with God? How have your wounds been instruments of healing in your own life? in the lives of others? Do you look upon your wounds as blessings or curses? In what ways have your wounds shaped your character and ongoing relationship with God?

2. The Pilgrim has a deep thirst for solitude. Do you make room in your life for solitude? Are you comfortable spending time alone? Are you uneasy with it? afraid of it? Are you able to listen to your heart? Can you delve into it? enter into it? listen to it? Can you rest within your heart and experience your spirit communing with the Spirit of the Lord? What practical steps can you take to highlight the contemplative dimension of your life?

3. The Pilgrim studies *The Philokalia* in great detail. Do you make room in your life for study? Do you devote any of your time during the day, the week, the month, to spiritual reading? Do you have a particular book or spiritual classic from which you derive much benefit? Do you test your own spiritual experiences against the wisdom of the Church's spiritual tradition? What connection is there between your spiritual reading and the rest of your life?

4. The Pilgrim receives a message from his *starets* in a dream. Do you pay attention to your dreams? Do you remember them? Have

any of your dreams ever made a deep impression on your conscious understanding of your relationship with others or with God? Do you ever listen to your dreams and try to understand what they are trying to say to you? Have you ever had the sense that God was trying to tell you something through your dreams? Do you believe that your dreams can sometimes hold the key for your further growth in the spiritual life? If so, how do you go about unlocking their meaning? Do you ever bring your dreams to others? Do you ask God for help in interpreting your dreams?

5.   As he leaves his small chapel post, the Pilgrim is subject to much scorn. Have you ever been ridiculed because of who you are or what you believe? What were the circumstances? Has it happened often in your life? How did you react? Are you ashamed of how you acted? grateful? Do you ask God for strength and courage to bear the troubles of life that pass your way? What does your suffering tell you about your relationship with Christ? Do you connect these troubles with the cross of Christ? Do you believe that Christ suffers with you when you suffer? Do you look upon your suffering as a type of witness? What has your suffering taught you about others? about God? about yourself?

6.   The Pilgrim experiences some concrete effects from his life of prayer. What are the concrete ramifications of prayer in your life? Have you noticed any physical, emotional, mental, or spiritual effects? Does your prayer life give you a sense of peace and a deeper awareness of the presence of God? Does it calm your emotions and bring you a sense of joy in carrying out the activities of the day? Does it bring you courage in the face of sickness and sorrow? Do you find that your prayer life helps you in what you are doing, enabling you to work more efficiently, to listen more attentively, to read with greater comprehension? If so, how would you explain these effects? Are they in any way tied to the particular form of prayer you use? Are they in any way tied to the Jesus Prayer?

7. Does the wandering Pilgrim's experience of God through the Jesus Prayer seem to be something within or beyond your reach? Do you look upon it as a practical means of attaining a deeper experience of God in the concrete circumstances of your life? Have you ever tried to imitate the Pilgrim's way of prayer? If not, what has kept you from doing so?

8. At one point, the Pilgrim finds it difficult to maintain a balance between prayer and action. How do you understand the relationship between action and contemplation in your life? Does action flow from contemplation? contemplation from action? Are they unrelated? Is there any tension between the two? If so, what is the tension like? Is it merely occasional and sporadic? Does it exist habitually, over long periods of time? Is it a positive or negative element in your spiritual life? Has this tension ever been problematic for you? If so, how have you tried to resolve it? What role has prayer played in easing this tension?

9. Have you, like the Pilgrim, ever found yourself in a situation where someone has turned to you for guidance in the spiritual life? What did you say? How did you react? In what ways did your own past experience prepare you for this moment? Do you think that these people came to you by chance? Can you see the hand of God at work in the lives of those you talked to? Do you think the Lord worked through you in these situations? In what ways did you hinder or help these people to deepen their prayer lives and thus come to a deeper awareness of the presence of God in their lives?

10. If you are actively involved in the ministry of spiritual direction, do you guide your directees toward solid spiritual teaching as found in the great Christian classics (for example, as in *The Philokalia*)? If so, do you also make the effort to explain whatever difficulties your directees may encounter when digesting the material they read? Are you able to simplify without compromising the

substance of the teaching? Are you able to translate the material in such a way that it touches the lives of your directees?

EXERCISES

1. Using any materials you wish (pencils, crayons, pastels, paints, etc.), draw a picture of yourself and the physical, psychological, and/or spiritual wounds that you have sustained during your life. Incorporate into this drawing not only the cause of these wounds but also the various persons who have been and will be affected by them (for example, family, friends, total strangers). When you have finished, take a good look at what you have drawn and ask yourself if the wounds you bear are deep or superficial, social or purely personal. Take your time with the picture. Think of it as a form of imaginative prayer that will bring you to a deeper understanding of yourself, others, and God. After doing so, take the drawing in your hands, close your eyes and, lifting it up to the Lord, ask Jesus to turn your wounds into an instrument of his healing love.

2. Find a book of spirituality that you have always wanted to read but never seemed to have time for. You may want to select *The Philokalia*, since it plays such a seminal role in the Pilgrim's own spiritual journey, but don't feel obliged. Devote a part of each day, perhaps a half an hour in the morning or the evening, for the next two weeks to read the book through. Try not to rush through it. Take more time if you need it. As you read, stop and meditate on those sections that strike you the most. Ask yourself how you would explain the book to a child. Try to simplify its teaching as much as possible without compromising it. When you have finished the book, tell someone about it. See if you can communicate the kernel of the book's teaching in as interesting, clear, and precise a way as possible.

3. Try to remember a recent dream that has made a deep impression on you. Write it out, including the plot, the main characters, and any symbols or images that seem to have particular significance. Once you have written it out, read it over a few times and ask yourself if you have left anything out. Then ask yourself if the dream is trying to say anything to you. Can you identify through it any of the conflicts or tensions of your conscious life? Which of the characters do you identify with the most? Which of them presents the greatest threat to you? Can you see a reflection of yourself in the other characters in your dream? Where is God in the dream? Is there a particular word or theme that sums up the message of the dream? Is the dream asking you to change in any way? Is it asking you to do something in particular? Do you take the dream seriously? If not, why not? If so, do you have sound reasons for thinking this way?

4. Starting with your earliest childhood memories, make up a list of all the people who have hurt you either knowingly or unknowingly. Try to be as comprehensive as possible, writing down their names if you know them, or a description of them and the circumstances in which the harm was done (for example, the older kids who made fun of you in the third grade, the friend who betrayed you in college, and so on). If this task seems too overbearing, scale down the time frame to suit your purposes (for example, those who have hurt you during the past year, the past month, the past week, and so on). Once you have drawn up the list, take a good look at it and try to picture each person and each situation. Then take the list with you to a quiet place where you can pray. Calm yourself. Be still in the presence of God. After reading each name on your list, recite the words of the Jesus Prayer. As you pray the words, let the image of the person pass through your mind and enter your heart. As you pray, ask the Lord to grant you the grace to extend and receive forgiveness. Continue onto the next name, doing the same until you have gone through the list. While doing so, remember that you yourself may very well be on someone else's list and that you

need to ask God's forgiveness for the times you have hurt others. Repeat the same process using a list, this time, of all the people *you* have hurt during your life. Don't forget to include those you have hurt without knowing it.

5. Think of a particular activity that you must do but do not like and have a particular distaste for. Whatever it is—be it physical, mental, or spiritual—try to infuse the activity with a contemplative dimension by invoking the name of Jesus as you do it. The use of the Jesus Prayer may be particularly helpful in this regard because its constant repetition brings our prayer beneath the level of conscious thought and allows the rhythm of our natural functions to be lifted up into the life of the Spirit. Try to bring this contemplative dimension to this and other activities that you have a difficult time with. Do not get discouraged if an integration between contemplation and action does not immediately occur. Patience may require a lifetime of quiet waiting for God to achieve what human effort alone cannot.

Narrative III
The Way of a Pilgrim

℘

J ust before leaving Irkutsk, I went to see my spiritual father, with whom I had so often talked, and I said to him, "Here I am actually off to Jerusalem. I have come to say goodbye and to thank you for your love for me in Christ, unworthy pilgrim as I am."

"May God bless your journey," he replied. "But how is it that you have never told me about yourself, who you are nor where you come from? I have heard a great deal about your travels, and I should be interested to know something about your birth and your life before you became a pilgrim."

"Why, very gladly," I answered. "I will tell you all about that also. It's not a very lengthy matter. I was born in a village in the government of Orel. After the death of our parents, there were just the two of us left—my brother and I. He was ten years old and I was two. We were adopted by our grandfather, a worthy old man and comfortably off. He kept an inn which stood on the main road and, thanks to his sheer goodness of heart, a lot of travelers put up there. My brother, who was a madcap child, spent most of his time running about in the village, but for my part, I liked better to stay near my grandfather. On Sundays and festivals, we used to go to church together and, at home, my grandfather often used to read the Bible, this very Bible here which now belongs to me. When my brother grew up, he took to drink. Once when I was seven years old and we were both of us lying down on the hearth, he pushed me so hard that I fell off and hurt my left arm, so that I have never been able to use it since; it is all withered up.

"My grandfather saw that I should never be fit to work on the land and taught me to read. As we had no spelling book, he did so from this Bible. He pointed out the A's, and made me form words and learn to know the letters when I saw them. I scarcely know how myself but, somehow, by saying things after him over and over again, I learned to read in the course of time. And later on, when my grandfather's sight grew weak, he often made me read the Bible aloud to him and he corrected me as he listened.

"There was a certain clerk who often came to our inn. He wrote a good hand and I liked watching him write. I copied his writing and he began to teach me. He gave me paper and ink; he made me quill pens, and so I learned to write also. Grandfather was very pleased and charged me thus: 'God has granted you the gift of learning; it will make a man of you. Give thanks to God and pray very often.'

"We used to attend all the services at church and we often had prayers at home. It was always my part to read Psalm 51 and, while I did so, Grandfather and Grandmother made their prostrations or knelt. When I was seventeen, I lost my grandmother. Then Grandfather said to me, 'This house of ours no longer has a mistress, and that is not well. Your brother is a worthless fellow. I am going to look for a wife for you; you must get married.' I was against the idea, saying that I was a cripple, but my grandfather would not give way. He found a worthy and sensible young girl about twenty years of age and I married her.

"A year later, my grandfather fell very ill. Knowing that his death was near, he called for me and bade me farewell, saying, 'I leave you my house and all I have. Obey your conscience, deceive no one and, above all, pray to God; everything comes from him.

Trust in him only. Go to church regularly, read your Bible, and remember me and your grandmother in your prayers. Here is my money, that also I give you; there is a thousand roubles. Take care of it. Do not waste it, but do not be miserly either. Give some of it to the poor and to God's church.' After this he died, and I buried him.

"My brother grew envious because the property had been left wholly to me. His anger against me grew, and the Enemy prompted him in this to such an extent that he even laid plans to kill me. In the end, this is what he did one night while we were asleep and no guests were in the house. He broke into the room where the money was kept, stole the money from a chest, and then set fire to the room. The fire had got a hold upon the whole building before we knew of it, and we only just escaped by jumping out of a window in our night clothes. The Bible was lying under our pillow, so we snatched it up and took it with us. As we watched our house burning, we said to one another, 'Thank God the Bible is saved; that at least is some consolation in our grief.' So everything we had was burnt, and my brother went off without a trace. Later on we heard that when he was in his cups he boasted of the fact that he had taken the money and burnt the house.

"We were left naked and ruined, absolutely beggars. We borrowed some money as best we could, built a little hut, and took up the life of landless peasants. My wife was clever with her hands. She knitted, spun, and sewed. People gave her jobs and, day and night, she worked and kept me. Owing to the uselessness of my arm, I could not even make bark shoes. She would do her knitting and spinning, and I would sit beside her and read the Bible. She would listen, and sometimes begin to cry. When I asked, 'What are you crying about? At least we are alive, thank God!' she would answer, 'It touches me so, that beautiful writing in the Bible.'

"Remembering what my grandfather had bidden us, we often fasted, every morning we said the Akathist hymn of our Lady, and at night we each made a thousand prostrations to avoid falling into temptation. Thus we lived quietly enough for two years.

"But this is what is so surprising—although we had no understanding of interior prayer offered in the heart and, indeed, had never heard of it, but prayed with the tongue only and made our prostrations without thought like buffoons turning somersaults; yet, in spite of all this, the wish for prayer was there, and the long prayers we said without understanding did not seem tiring; indeed, we liked them. Clearly it is true, as a certain teacher once told me, that a secret prayer lies hidden within the human heart. The man himself does not know it. Yet, working mysteriously within his soul, it urges him to prayer according to each man's knowledge and power.

"After two years of this sort of life that we were leading, my wife was taken suddenly ill with a high fever. She was given her Communion and on the ninth day of her illness she died. I was now left entirely alone in the world. There was no sort of work that I could do; still I had to live, and it went against my conscience to beg. Besides that, I felt such grief at the loss of my wife that I did not know what to do with myself. When I happened to go into our little hut and caught sight of her clothes or perhaps a scarf, I burst into tears and even fell down senseless. So, feeling I could no longer bear my grief living at home, I sold the hut for twenty roubles, and such clothes as there were of my own and my wife's I gave away to the poor. Because of my crippled arm, I was given a passport which set me free once for all from public duties and, taking my beloved Bible, I set straight off, without caring or thinking where I was going.

"But after a while I began to think where I would go and said to myself, 'First of all I will go to Kiev. I will venerate the shrines of those who were pleasing to God and ask for their help in my trouble.' As soon as I had made up my mind to this, I began to feel better and, a good deal comforted, I made my way to Kiev. Since that time, for the last thirteen years that is, I have gone on wandering from place to place. I have made the round of many churches and monasteries but, nowadays, I am taking more and more to wandering over the steppes and fields. I do not know whether God will vouchsafe to let me go to Jerusalem. If it be his will, when the time comes, my sinful bones may be laid to rest there."

"And how old are you?"

"Thirty-three."

"Well, dear Brother, you have reached the age of our Lord Jesus Christ!"

Commentary III

Our Spiritual Legacy

"But how is it that you have never told me about yourself,
who you are nor where you come from?"

FROM *THE WAY OF A PILGRIM*

૪૭

T he third narrative is the shortest of the four that make up *The Way of a Pilgrim* and contains the author's reflections on his early life. Just before setting out for Odessa, the first leg of his journey to the Holy Land, the Pilgrim visits his spiritual father[37] to say goodbye to him and to thank him for the many kindnesses he has received from his hands. Upon doing so, he is asked to say something about were he comes from and what his life was like before becoming a pilgrim. Our anonymous author is more than happy to comply.

SUFFERING FOR A LIFETIME

Summary
The Pilgrim says that he was born in a village of the Orel province. After his parents died when he was two years old, he and his ten-year-old brother were taken in and raised by his grandparents. The

Pilgrim describes his grandfather as an honest, God-fearing man, who attended church regularly, read the Bible often, and was kind to the travelers who stopped at the inn he owned on the main road of town. He tells of the troubles his older brother had in his adolescent life, of how he took to drinking and carousing, and of how he was a cause of ceaseless worry and concern to his grandfather. He also relates how, at seven years of age, he himself was pushed off the hearth by his older brother and, as a result, permanently lost the use of his left hand. The Pilgrim then tells how his grandfather, realizing that a withered hand would prevent his grandson from doing manual labor when he was older, used the family Bible to teach him how to read. A district clerk was also hired to teach him how to write.

His grandmother died when he was seventeen, and his grandfather grew intent on his grandson marrying. A wedding was arranged for him with a mature girl of twenty years of age. Together, they lived a happy and devout life with his grandfather and inherited everything from him when he died one year later.

The Pilgrim then recounts vengeful actions of his brother, who was left out of the inheritance because of his reckless living. One night, the brother broke in to the inn, stole all their money, and set fire to the structure. The poor Pilgrim and his wife escaped with nothing but the family Bible, which they kept under their pillow. Completely destitute and needing to start all over again, they managed to borrow money to build a small cottage, and they earned their keep as landless peasants, supporting themselves on the wife's weaving, spinning, and sewing. Since he was unable to work on account of his withered left hand, the Pilgrim tells how he sat beside his wife and read the Bible to her as she worked. Although they lived a simple, frugal life, they were devout and happy. They fasted frequently, chanted the Akathist hymn to Mary the Mother of God every morning, and did many prostrations before going to bed.

After two years, the Pilgrim's wife suddenly became ill with a high fever and died, after receiving her last Communion on the ninth day of her illness. Now completely alone and with no means of supporting himself, the Pilgrim was quite distraught and over-whelmed with grief. Whenever he walked into his cottage and saw his wife's clothing or the kerchief she wore, he would let out a heartrending cry and, at times, even faint.

His sense of grief eventually got to be too much for him, so he sold his cabin for twenty roubles and gave to the poor whatever was left of his wife's clothing. He explains how, because of his disabled hand, he was able to obtain a disability passport and how, with his Bible in hand, he set out on a life of wandering with no specific destination in mind. In time, he set out for Kiev in order to venerate the relics of the saints and to ask for their help and intercession.

The Pilgrim tells his spiritual father that this was thirteen years ago and that he has wandered through different places and visited many churches and monasteries since that time. He goes on to tell him that now, at the age of thirty-three, the age of Jesus Christ when he died, he is not sure if God has ordained him to reach the holy city of Jerusalem. He ends the third narrative with the conjecture that, if it is the Lord's will, perhaps it is time for his sinful bones to be buried there.

Reflection

A number of important insights arise from the author's brief ac-count of his early years. One is how he deals with his suffering. First, although a long series of tragedies besets him and takes its damaging toll, he does not give in to despair or lose hope. He is orphaned at the age of two; he loses the use of his left hand at the age of seven; he loses both grandparents in the space of a year; he is robbed and burned out of house and home by his brother; and he loses his wife some two years later. By the time he is twenty years old, the Pilgrim has suffered enough for an entire lifetime. Still, he is not bitter. He has been raised by his grandfather to be grateful for the events that come his way and to believe that with the Lord "all things work for good" (Rom 8:28).

And indeed they do. The Pilgrim is orphaned, but raised by his grandparents in an atmosphere of love and support. He is wounded for life at an early age, but learns to read and write as a result. He loses his grandmother, but marries a devout and loving woman. He loses home and fortune, but manages to save the family Bible and exclaim with his wife: "Thank God, the Bible is saved; that at least is some consolation in our grief."[38] He loses his wife to illness but, free from all family ties, is able to embark on a life of wandering and learning of the secrets of ceaseless prayer.

The Pilgrim, of course, relates all of this in hindsight and it is, therefore, difficult for us to determine his immediate reaction to the events as they occurred. Still, when asked to recount the events of his early life some thirteen years later, he does not try to repress the tragic events that occurred. On the contrary, it is in the midst of his misfortunes that he has found the gentle, guiding hand of God. This indicates that the Pilgrim has come to terms with his past. He has sifted through his memories and has put them together in such a way that they convey the experience of faith that sustained him then—and which continues to sustain him. In a similar way, spiritual directors should encourage their directees to sift through their earlier lives and confront the darkness they find there. Only by doing so will they be able to let go of the pain they may still carry and, like the Pilgrim, be able to find the hand of God guiding them and moving them forward.

Second, the painful incidents with his older brother reveal a certain amount of dysfunction in the Pilgrim's immediate family. It is difficult to say just where this came from: a traumatic reaction to the loss of their parents at such young ages (two and ten years of age), difficulties on the part of the older brother in adapting to life with his grandparents; perhaps some deeper psychological cause. Whatever, the Pilgrim recognizes in hindsight that something went wrong in his brother's life and that his heavy drinking was a symptom of something deeper. What is interesting in this part of the story is that the Pilgrim recognizes the darkness in his family life and his helplessness to do anything about it. He never retaliates against his brother but, instead, prays for him, as any Christian should.

The Pilgrim's honesty about his family background reminds us that God calls all of us to become saints and that very few of us have led lives sheltered from the harshness of sin and the world's malice. More often than not it is within the dysfunctional relationships within our own family where we first experience the cold indifference and, at times, outright hostility that mars so much of the world's activity. This realistic picture painted by the author endears him to us, his readers, because if we are honest with ourselves and take an honest look at our own family background, we will recognize dysfunctional patterns in our own lives. As far as spiritual direction is concerned, directors should encourage their directees to look back at their family of origin to uncover and talk about whatever dysfunctional relationships they find there. Only by taking a good hard look at these relationships and the toll they have taken in their lives will they be able to let go of them and carry on with life.

Third, the Pilgrim's dysfunctional relationship with his brother turns out to be both a blessing and a curse. It is a blessing because were it not for his withered hand and the loss of his property, the Pilgrim would probably never have been moved to take up the life of wandering and to delve into the mysteries of the Jesus Prayer. It is a curse because for the rest of his life he must bear the wound inflicted on him by his brother.

It is easy for us to forget that the Pilgrim is a wounded traveler. Although he accepts his handicap with extraordinary resignation, he must, nevertheless, bear the wound and the memory of its cause with him wherever he goes. This wound reminds the Pilgrim, and us, that no one ever fully escapes the past. The wound is a vivid reminder of his brother's hatred, which he carries with him wherever he goes. Even though time, prayer and, above all, the grace of God will bring about a healing of memories and even genuine forgiveness on the part of the victim, the physical scar of the withered limb is a harsh physical reminder of the world's need of redemption.

This wound, however, is more than a mere reminder; it also provides opportunities for the Pilgrim's growth in other ways: intellectually, by the subsequent chances he receives to learn to read and write—skills we are led to conclude he never would have developed had it not been for his disability; and spiritually, by virtue of the interior journey he takes to the secrets of the interior prayer of the heart—a way of praying he probably never would have had the opportunity to become acquainted with. What is more, the Pilgrim's positive response to these challenges for growth make him a much more sensitive and caring person, one who is able to listen to the concerns of others and respond to their needs in loving and appropriate ways. When it comes to spiritual direction, directors should help their directees look at the wounds—physical, emotional, mental, spiritual, and social—that they have been carrying around with them for most of their lives. When doing so, directors should help directees look at the causes of these wounds and ask themselves what opportunities for growth these wounds represent.

Fourth, although the Pilgrim knew nothing at all of the Jesus Prayer during this period of his life, it is clear from the start that he was nurtured in an atmosphere of deep and endearing faith in his grandparents' home. The centerpiece of that faith is the Bible. Through this book the Pilgrim learns not only to read and write but also to delve into the mysteries of the faith. This book is with him at every stage of his life and will be with him till the end. In many ways, the Pilgrim's entire story is one of how he comes to a deeper and deeper appreciation of the mysteries of this holy book. In this respect, *The Philokalia* and the *starets* are nothing more than means by which he comes to a deeper and more enriching understanding of the living Word of God. By recognizing the presence of this Word in his life from the earliest times, the Pilgrim affirms his belief in God's providential care. Although he can smile at the way he and his wife made prostrations without thought, "like buffoons turning somersaults,"[39] he realizes that such prayers were from the heart and were motivated by a deep desire to pray. From this perspective, the Pilgrim sees that God was preparing him for the graces of interior prayer long before he ever walked into church on the twenty-fourth Sunday after Pentecost and heard the words of 1 Thessalonians 5:17 about unceasing prayer. In like manner, spiritual directors should encourage their directees to look at the events and people who have nurtured their life of prayer and have given them a deeper appreciation of the presence of God's Word. Often it is only in hindsight that we are able to gain enough perspective on life to truly appreciate what has taken place.

Finally, finding this recollection of the author's early life in a book, itself an account of his own spiritual development, amounts to having an autobiographical reflection *within* an autobiographical reflection. The author has structured his account in such a way that recounting his life's story is highlighted as a major way in which he is able to understand the movement of God in his life—just as we might better understand the movement of God in our life in the recounting of our own life story. We can well imagine the Pilgrim having recounted this tale of his early years many times in his life and, chances are, he is asked to do so again as he makes his way toward Jerusalem. Each time would be similar but different, alike but unique, because as the Pilgrim becomes more and more adept at reading the mysteries of the Bible and the language of creation, he also becomes more and more versed in the language of life—and death. The closing parallel between the Pilgrim and Jesus at the end of the narrative, and the fact that he too is about to make his way toward Jerusalem, verifies this claim and shows that the Pilgrim's story—as is ours—is intimately related to Jesus' own.

Closely allied to this dynamic is the attentive listening of the spiritual father who allows the Pilgrim to tell his story in his own time and at his own pace. Every tale needs a hearer; every story needs an active listener; every speaker needs someone willing to lend an ear. When viewed in this light, this third narrative incorporates into the text itself an active conversation of reflective recounting and holy listening between the Pilgrim and his spiritual father—

qualities that go to the core of good spiritual direction. Directors should seek to create an atmosphere where both these qualities can be duly fostered in their own lives and in those they direct. Otherwise, they run the risk of making direction something abstract and without concrete application to the circumstances of their directees' daily lives.

CONCLUSION

The third narrative constitutes a break with the previous two in that it goes back to an earlier time, before the events in either Narrative I or Narrative II ever took place, to look at what the Pilgrim's life was like before he was a pilgrim and before he knew anything about the Jesus Prayer.

This reflective movement backwards, however, is also a movement forward. The Pilgrim, we must remember, is about to begin another journey, not to Kiev or Irkutsk, but to the Holy City—Jerusalem. Because this journey will probably be the most difficult he will ever undertake, it is important for him, at the outset, to look back at his life to make an account of things, to put them in order. If he does not do that at this point, he may never get another chance. He himself hints to his spiritual father that he is not sure he will ever arrive or ever return. As he sets out, therefore, it is essential that he have a clear idea of where he has come from and why he is making the journey.

The third narrative does just that for the Pilgrim; it provides a cathartic experience for him, one that enables him to remember, to let go, and to move on. By recounting the story of his early life, the Pilgrim gets to recount one last time before his departure those important moments of his past that have shaped his life and, to a large extent, have brought him to where he is at that point. In order to go on with his journey, the Pilgrim must first move backwards, not in distance, but in time. He must go back to an earlier time and, through the power of selection, recount the tale in a way that makes the most sense to him in the context of his present life situation. In this third narrative, the "way of the Pilgrim" reflects most closely the way of a person in search of spiritual guidance. This focus on reflection binds the two ways closely together, so much so that they can be separated only with great difficulty.

REFLECTION QUESTIONS

1. Unforeseen circumstances delay the Pilgrim's journey to Jerusalem. How do you react when unexpected circumstances force you to change your plans? Do you get upset? vengeful? Do you express your anger by taking it out on those around you? Do you look for the quickest way to put your original plans back on track, or do you go with the flow? Do you welcome the unexpected as an opportunity to encounter the elusive presence of God in your life? What does your reaction to the unexpected tell you about yourself and your relationship to God and others?

2. The Pilgrim's story reveals that he has a thorny relationship with his older brother. Do you have strained relationships with any of your family members? If so, what is the origin of the tension? Would you describe any of these relationships as dysfunctional? What effects have these relationships had on the rest of your family? Have you in any way been responsible for the strain in the relationships? What can you do to improve the situation? Do you pray for these difficult family members? Do you pray for your family? Do you ask God for help in the matter?

3. The wounds inflicted upon us by our family members cut deeply and often stay with us for our entire lives. Have you, like the Pilgrim, been hurt deeply by a family member? What is the nature of the wound? Do you think about it often? How has the wound af-

fected the way you live your life? How has it affected the way you relate to others? to God? Has any good come from it? any evil? Have you inflicted similar wounds on others? If so, have you asked their forgiveness? What else could you do to remedy the situation?

4. After losing nearly all their personal possessions in a fire set by a family member (the Pilgrim's older brother), the Pilgrim and his wife give thanks to God for not having lost their family Bible. How attached are you to your possessions, material or otherwise? How would *you* react if something similar happened to you? Would you be able to give honor and thanks to God even in the midst of grave personal loss? Would you turn to the Bible for spiritual support and nourishment?

5. At one point in his story, the Pilgrim relates how foolish he and his wife must have looked in their early attempts at prayer. Have you ever examined the history of how you pray? If not, what keeps you from doing so? If so, what changes have you noticed? Do you find that at certain periods of your life you have favored one form of prayer over another? Is there a particular form of prayer you feel most drawn to? Is there anything you would like to change now?

6. After his wife's death, the Pilgrim goes through a period of mourning and eventually sets out on a life of pilgrimage. How have you reacted at the loss of someone close to you? Did you hide your grieving from others? Did you express your grief? Did you distance yourself from it? Did you allow it to overwhelm you? Did it bring new direction and purpose to your life? Do you carry the love of those you have lost with you throughout the rest of your pilgrimage through life?

7. Nearly the whole of Narrative III consists of the Pilgrim's re-flection on his early life. To what extent has your childhood and early adulthood shaped the course of your later years? Do you often

look back to these early periods? Have you ever written down your thoughts? Has your interpretation of the events changed over time? Have you been able to see the hand of God at work in these early periods? If so, in what ways? Have you ever told the story of your early life to someone else?

8. The Pilgrim's story shows that some key events (for example, loss of the use of his left hand, the fire set by his brother, the death of his wife) changed the course of his life. Looking back on your entire life, what would you mark as the key events? How have those events changed your life? Did they do so for the better or for the worse? Do you have any regrets about how your life has evolved? Would you change anything—either in the past or the present— in your life if you could?

9. This narrative highlights not only the Pilgrim's autobiographical reflection but also the active listening of his spiritual father. Are you a good listener? When you are engaged in conversation, do you truly listen to what the other person is saying or do you simply wait for a convenient pause so that you can interject your own opinion? How can you improve your listening skills? What can you do to help others share their life stories with you more freely?

10. This narrative bears a close resemblance to a session of spiritual direction. If you are a spiritual director, to what extent do you encourage your directees to delve into their past experiences? Are you willing to delve beneath the surface of things with them? Have you established a relationship of trust that allows your directees to share their deeply personal and often painful experiences with you? Do you share your own personal experiences with them at appropriate times? Do you interpret their experiences *for* them or do you try to help them uncover the meaning of their lives for themselves?

EXERCISES

1. Draw up a family tree, starting with your immediate family members and working your way out to extended family connections. Be as comprehensive as possible. Include both the living and the dead, those you have met and those you have not met. Go back as far as your memory allows. When you finish, examine the names on the list and ask yourself if any tension exists between you and them. Circle the names of those with whom you experience tension, using an array of colors to distinguish the more strained relationships from the lesser ones. Then go back over the list and, one by one, picture each of the people whose names you have circled. Recite the Jesus Prayer as you pass from name to name, asking the Lord to mediate in the relationship and to heal the broken bonds of kinship between you and the other.

2. Take an inventory of your life, including your relationships, material possessions, special talents, successes, and dreams. Prioritize the items by placing that which you would least like to part with at the top of the list, and that which you could most easily part with at the bottom of the list. When you finish this task, cross out each item, starting at the bottom of the list and slowly moving toward the top. As you delete each item, close your eyes and ask the Lord to give you the grace not to hold on tightly to this particular good and to be ready and able to let go of it if asked. When you finish this exercise, pray the Jesus Prayer, asking the Lord to help you maintain a proper perspective on life.

3. Starting from your earliest memories and making your way to the present day, draw up a list of events that have had the greatest impact on your life. Go back over each of these events and write out both a description of what happened and a corresponding explanation of why it has had such a great impact on your life. Carefully read over what you have written to see if you have left anything out.

Then try to imagine all the possible circumstances that could have changed these events and thus the outcome of your life. After doing this, go back over your list and, next to each item, write "Yes" or "No" in answer to this one simple question: "God's hand was somehow present in this key event of my life." At the end of this exercise ask yourself if God seemed more *present* to you or *absent* at these key moments of your life. Then pray the Jesus Prayer several times, asking the Lord to help you to remain faithful even during difficult times.

4. "We know that all things work together for good for those who love God, who are called according to his purpose" (Rom 8:28). Look back over the misfortunes that have come your way in life, especially those that seemed to have no redeeming purpose. Select one misfortune in particular and spend time thinking about it and praying over it, asking the Lord to show you what, if any, good has come from it. Then list what some of the positive results might have been. If nothing comes to mind, ask the Lord to help you trust in the truth of the apostle's words. Carry the memory of that event with you through the day, and recite the Jesus Prayer whenever the memory of that event passes through your mind.

5. Spend a few moments in a quiet place. Listen to the sounds outside of you, around you, and within you. Try to be an active listener to all that is going on in the present moment. Ask the Lord to help you listen to and respond to the still small voice of the Spirit in your heart. Ask God to help you listen to that voice in the events of the day and in the people you meet. Ask God to help you be an active listener for others. As you leave this quiet place, ask the Lord to help you listen before you speak. Resolve to practice this form of active listening with the very next person you meet. If you are a spiritual director, resolve to carry on this practice of active listening with your directees.

The Way of a Pilgrim

"But it is good for me to hold me fast by God, to put my trust in the Lord God."

ॐ

"T he Russian proverb is true, which says that 'man proposes but God disposes,'" said I, as I came back again to my spiritual father. "I thought that by now I should certainly be on my way to Jerusalem. But see how differently things have fallen out. Something quite unlooked for has happened and kept me in the same place here for another three days. And I could not help coming to tell you about it and to ask your advice in making up my mind about the matter."

It happened like this. I had said goodbye to everybody and, with God's help, started on my way. I had gotten as far as the outskirts of the town when I saw a man I knew standing at the door of the very last house. He was at one time a pilgrim like me, but I had not seen him for about three years. We greeted one another and he asked me where I was going. "God willing," I answered, "I want to go to Jerusalem."

"Thank God! There is a nice fellow traveler for you," he said.

"God be with you and with him, too," said I, "but surely you know that it is never my way to travel with other people. I always wander about alone."

"Yes, but listen. I feel sure that this one is just your sort; you will suit each other down to the ground. Now look here, the father of the master of this house, where I have been taken on as a servant, is going under a vow to Jerusalem, and you will easily get used to each other. He belongs to this town. He's a good old man and, what's more, he is quite deaf—so much so that however much you shout, he can't hear a word. If you want to ask him anything you have to write it on a bit of paper, and then he answers.

"So you see, he won't bore you on the road; he won't speak to you. Even at home here he grows more and more silent. On the other hand, you will be a great help to him on the way. His son is giving him a horse and cart, which he will take as far as Odessa and then sell there. The old man wants to go on foot, but the horse is going as well because he has a bit of luggage and some things he is taking to the Lord's tomb. And you can put your knapsack in with them too, of course. Now just think, how can we possibly send an old deaf man off with a horse, all by himself, on such a long journey? They have searched and searched for somebody to take him, but they all want to be paid such a lot. Besides, there's a risk in sending him with someone we don't know, for he has money and belongings with him. Say 'Yes,' Brother. It will really be all right. Make up your mind now for the glory of God and the love of your neighbor. I will vouch for you to his people, and they will be too pleased for words; they are kindly folk and very fond of me. I've been working for them for two years now."

All this talk had taken place at the door, and he now took me into the house. The head of the household was there, and I saw clearly that they were quite a worthy and decent family. So I agreed to the plan. So now we have arranged to start with God's blessing, after hearing the liturgy two days after Christmas. What unexpected things we meet with on life's journey! Yet all the while, God and his holy providence guide our actions and overrule our plans, as it is written, "*It is God which works in you both to will and to do.*"

On hearing all this, my spiritual father said, "I rejoice with all my heart, dear Brother, that God has so ordered it that I should see you again, so unexpectedly and so soon. And since you now have time, I want, in all love, to keep you a little longer, and you shall tell me more about the instructive experiences you have met with in the course of your long pilgrimages. I have already listened with great pleasure and interest to what you told me before."

"I am quite ready and happy to do that," I answered, and I began, as follows:

A great many things have happened to me—some good and some bad. It would take a long while to tell of them all, and much I have already forgotten. For I have tried especially to remember only such matters as guided and urged my idle soul to prayer. All the rest I rarely remember or, rather, I have tried to forget the past, as Saint Paul bids us when he says, *"Forgetting the things that are behind and stretching forward to the things that are before, I press on toward the goal of the prize of the high calling."* My late *starets* of blessed memory also used to say that the forces which are against prayer in the heart attack us from two sides: from the left hand and from the right. That is to say, if the enemy cannot turn us from prayer by means of vain thoughts and sinful ideas, then he brings back into our minds good things we have been taught and fills us with beautiful ideas, so that one way or another he may lure us away from prayer, which is a thing he cannot bear. It is called "a theft from the right-hand side," and in it the soul, putting aside its converse with God, turns to the satisfaction of converse with self or with created things. He taught me, therefore, not to admit during times of prayer even the most lofty of spiritual thoughts. And if I saw that in the course of the day time had been spent more in improving thought and talk than in the actual hidden prayer of the heart, then I was to think of it as a loss of the sense of proportion or a sign of spiritual greed. This is above all true, he said, in the case of beginners, for whom it is most needful that time given to prayer should be very much more than that taken up by other sides of the devout life.

Still, one cannot forget everything. A matter may have printed itself so deeply in one's mind that, although it has not been actually thought of for a long time, yet it is remembered very clearly. A case in point is the few days' stay that God deemed me worthy to enjoy with a certain devout family in the following manner.

During my wanderings in the Tobolsk province, I happened to pass through a certain country town. My supply of dried bread had run very low, so I went to one of the houses to ask for some more. The householder said, "Thank God, you have come just at the right moment. My wife has only just taken the bread out of the oven, so there is a hot loaf for you. Remember me in your prayers." I thanked him and was putting the bread away in my knapsack when his wife, who was looking on, said, "What a wretched state your knapsack is in; it is all worn out. I'll give you another instead." And she gave me a good strong one. I thanked them very heartily and went on. On leaving the town I went into a little shop to ask for a bit of salt, and the shopkeeper gave me a small bag quite full. I rejoiced in spirit and thanked God for leading me, unworthy as I was, to such kindly folk. "Now," thought I, "without having to worry about food, I shall be filled and content for a whole week. Bless the Lord, O my soul!"

Three miles or so from this town, the road I was following passed through a poor village where I saw a little wooden church nicely decked out and painted on the outside. As I was going by it, I felt a wish to honor God's house and, going onto the porch, I prayed for a while. On the grass at the side of the church there were playing two little children of five or six years of age. I took them to be the parish priest's children, for they were very nicely dressed. I finished my prayers and went on my way, but I had not gone a dozen paces from the church when I heard a shout behind me. "Dear little beggar! Dear little beggar! Stop!" The two little ones I had seen, a boy and a girl, were calling and running after me. I stopped and they ran up to me and took me by the hand. "Come along to Mummy. She likes beggars."

"I'm not a beggar," I told them, "I'm just a passerby."

"Why have you got a bag then?"

"That is for the bread I eat on the way."

"All the same, you must come. Mummy will give you some money for your journey."

"But where is your mummy?" I asked.

"Down there behind the church, behind that little wood."

They took me into a beautiful garden in the middle of which stood a large country house. We went inside, and how clean and smart it all was! The lady of the house comes hurrying to us.

"Come, welcome! God has sent you to us, and how did you come? Sit down, sit down." With her own hands she took off my knapsack and put it on a table, and made me sit in a very comfortably padded chair. "Wouldn't you like something to eat? Or a cup of tea? Isn't there anything you need?"

"I most humbly thank you," I answered, "but I have a whole bagful of food. It is true that I do take tea, but as a peasant I am not very used to it. I value your heartfelt and kindly welcome even more than the treat you offer me. I shall pray that God may bless you for showing such love for strangers in the spirit of the Gospels."

While I was speaking, a strong feeling came over me, urging me to withdraw within myself again. The Prayer was surging up in my heart, and I needed peace and silence to give free play to this quickening flame of prayer, as well as to hide from others the outward signs which went with it, such as tears and sighs and unusual movements of the face and lips. I therefore got up, saying, "Please excuse me, but I must leave now. May the Lord Jesus Christ be with you and with your dear little children."

"Oh, no! God forbid that you should go away. I won't allow it. My husband, who is a magistrate, will be coming back from town this evening, and how delighted he will be to see you! He reverences every pilgrim as a messenger of God. If you go away, he will be really grieved not to have seen you. Besides that, tomorrow is Sunday, and you will pray with us at the liturgy, and at the dinner table take your share with us in what God has sent. On holy days we always have up to thirty guests, and all of them our poor brothers in Jesus Christ. Come now, why have you told me nothing about yourself—where you come from and where you are going? Talk to me. I like listening to the spiritual conversation of devout people. Children, Children! Take the pilgrim's knapsack into the oratory; he will spend the night there."

I was astonished as I listened to what she said, and I asked myself whether I was talking with a human being or with a ghost of some sort.

So I stayed and waited for her husband. I gave her a short account of my travels and said I was on my way to Irkutsk. "Why, then you will have to go through Tobolsk," said the lady, "and my own mother is a nun in a convent there. She is a *skhimnitsa*[40] now. We will give you a letter and she will be glad to see you. A great many people go to consult her on spiritual matters. And you will be able to take her a book by Saint John of the Ladder which we have just ordered from Moscow at her request. How nicely it all fits in!"

Soon it was dinnertime, and we sat down to table. Four other ladies came in and began the meal with us. When the first course was ended, one of them rose, bowed to the icon,[41] and then to us. Then she went and fetched the second course and sat down again. Then another of the ladies in the same way went and brought the third course. When I saw this, I said to my hostess, "May I venture to ask whether these ladies are relations of yours?"

"Yes, they are indeed sisters to me; this is my cook and this the coachman's wife; that one has charge of the keys and the other is my maid. They are all married. I have no unmarried girls at all in my whole household."

The more I saw and heard of all this, the more surprised I was, and I thanked God for letting me see these devout people. I felt the prayer stirring strongly in my heart, so wishing to be alone as soon as I could and not hinder the prayer, I said to the lady as soon as we rose from the table, "No doubt you will rest for a while after dinner; and I am so used to walking that I will go for a stroll in the garden."

"No, I don't rest," she replied. "I will come into the garden with you, and you shall talk to me about something instructive. If you go alone, the children will give you no peace; directly they see you, they will not leave you for a minute. They are so fond of beggars and brothers in Christ and pilgrims."

There was nothing for me to do but to go with her. In order to avoid doing the talking myself, when we got into the garden, I bowed down to the ground before her and said, "Do tell me, please, have you lived this devout life long and how did you come to take it up?"

"I will tell you the whole story if you like," was the answer. "You see, my mother was a great-granddaughter of Saint Joasaph, whose relics rest at Byelograd. We had a large town house, one wing of which was rented to a man who was a gentleman but not well off. After a while, he died; his wife was left pregnant and herself died in giving birth to a child. The infant was left an orphan and in poverty and, out of pity, my mother adopted him. A year later, I was born. We grew up together and did lessons together with the same tutors and governesses, and were as used to each other as a real brother and sister. Some while later, my father died, and my mother gave up living in town and came with us to live on this estate of hers here. When we grew up, she gave me in marriage to her adopted son, settled this estate on us, and herself took the veil in a convent, where she had a cell built for her. She gave us a mother's blessing and, as her last will and testament, she urged us to live as good Christians, to say our prayers fervently, and above all try to fulfill the greatest of God's commandments—that is, the love of one's neighbor, to feed and help our poor brothers in Christ in simplicity and humility, to bring up our children in the fear of the Lord, and to treat our serfs as our brothers. And that is how we have been living here by ourselves for the last ten years now, trying as best we could to carry out Mother's last wishes. We have a guest house for beggars and, at the present moment, there are living in it more than ten crippled and sick people. If you care to, we will go and see them tomorrow."

When she had ended her story, I asked her where the book by Saint John of the Ladder was, which she wished to send to her mother. "Come indoors," she said, "and I will find it for you."

We had just sat down and begun to read it when her husband came in and, seeing me, gave me a warm welcome. We kissed each other as two brothers in Christ, and then he took me off to his own room, saying, "Come, dear Brother, let us go into my study and you shall bless my cell. I expect she (pointing to his wife) has been boring you. No sooner does she catch sight of a pilgrim of either sex, or of some sick person, than she is so delighted that she will not leave them day or night. She has been like that for years and years."

We went into the study. What a lot of 'books there were, and beautiful icons, and the life-giving cross with the figure life-sized, and the Gospels lying near it! I said a prayer, and then, "You are in God's own paradise here," I said. "Here is the Lord Jesus Christ himself, and his most holy Mother, and the blessed saints! And there," I went on, pointing to the books, "are the divine, living, and ever-lasting words of their teaching. I expect you very often enjoy heavenly converse with them."

"Yes, I admit I am a great lover of reading," he answered.

"What sort of books are they you have here?" I asked.

"I have a large number of religious books," was the answer. "Here you see are the Lives of the Saints for the whole year, and the works of Saint John Chrysostom and Basil the Great and many other theologians and philosophers. I have a lot of volumes of sermons, too, by celebrated modern preachers. My library is worth about five hundred pounds."

"Haven't you anything on prayer?"

"Yes, I am very fond of reading about prayer. Here is the very latest work on the subject, the work of a Petersburg priest." He took down a book on the Lord's Prayer and we began to read it with great enjoyment. A short while after, the lady came in bringing tea, followed by the children, who dragged in a large silver basket full of biscuits and cakes such as I had never tasted before in my life.

My host took the book from me and handed it to his wife, saying, "Now we will get her to read; she reads beautifully, and we will keep our strength up with the tea."

So she began reading and we listened. And as I listened, I felt the action of the Prayer in my heart. The longer the reading went on, the more the Prayer grew and made me glad. Suddenly, I saw something flash quickly before my eyes, in the air as it were, like the figure of my departed *starets*. I started, and so as to hide the fact, I said, "Excuse me, I must have dropped asleep for a moment." Then I felt as though the soul of my *starets* made its way into my own, or gave light to it. I felt a sort of light in my mind, and a number of ideas about prayer came to me. I was just crossing myself and setting my will to put these ideas aside when the lady came to the end of the book and her husband asked me whether I had liked it, so that talking began again. "Very much," I answered. "The 'Our Father' is the loftiest and most precious of all the written prayers we Christians have, for the Lord Jesus Christ Himself gave it to us. And the explanation of it which has just been read is very good, too, only it all deals, for the most part, with the active side of the Christian life, and in my reading of the holy Fathers, I have come across a more speculative and mystical explanation of the prayer."

"In which of the Fathers did you read this?"

"Well, in Maximus the Confessor, for example, and in Peter the Damascene, in *The Philokalia.*"

"Do you remember it? Tell us about it, please."

"Certainly. The first words of the prayer, 'Our Father which art in heaven' are explained in your book as a call to brotherly love for one's neighbor, since we are all children of the one Father—and that is very true. But in the holy Fathers, the explanation goes further and is more deeply spiritual. They say that when we use these words, we should lift up our mind to heaven, to the heavenly Father, and remember every moment that we are in the presence of God.

"The words 'Hallowed be Thy name' are explained in your book by the care we ought to have not to utter the name of God except with reverence, nor to use it in a false oath, in a word that the holy name of God be spoken reverently and not taken in vain. But the mystical writers see here a plain call to inward prayer of the heart; that is, that the most holy name of God may be stamped inwardly upon the heart and be hallowed by self-acting prayer and hallow all our feelings and all the powers of the soul. The words 'Thy kingdom come,' they explain thus—may inward peace and quiet and spiritual joy come to our hearts. In your book again, the words 'Give us this day our daily bread' are understood as asking for what we need for our bodily life, not for more than that, but for what is needed for ourselves and for the help of our neighbor. On the other hand, Maximus the Confessor understands by 'daily bread' the feeding of the soul with heavenly bread, that is, the Word of God and the union of the soul with God, by dwelling upon him in thought and the unceasing inward prayer of the heart."

"But the attainment of interior prayer is a very big business and almost impossible for lay folk," exclaimed my host. "We are lucky if we manage to say our ordinary prayers without slothfulness."

"Don't look at it in that way," said I. "If it were out of the question and quite too hard to do, God would not have bidden us all do it. His strength is made perfect in weakness. The holy Fathers, who speak from their own experience, offer us the means and make the way to win the prayer of the heart easier. Of course, for hermits, they give special and higher methods, but for those who live in the world, their writings show ways which truly lead to interior prayer."

"I have never come across anything of that sort in my reading," he said.

"If you would care to hear it, may I read you a little from *The Philokalia?*" I asked, taking up my copy. I found the section by Peter the Damascene and read as follows: " 'One must learn to call upon the name of God, more even than breathing—at all times, in all places, in every kind of occupation. The apostle says, *"Pray without ceasing."* That is, he teaches men to have the remembrance of God in all times and places and circumstances. If you are making something, you must call to mind the Creator of all things; if you see the light, remember the Giver of it; if you see the heavens and the earth and the sea and all that is in them, wonder and praise the Maker of them. If you put on your clothes, recall whose gift they are and thank him who provides for your life. In short, let every action be a cause of your remembering and praising God and, lo, you will be praying without ceasing and therein your soul will always rejoice.' There, you see, this way of ceaseless prayer is simple and easy and within the reach of everybody so long as he has some amount of human feeling."

They were extraordinarily pleased with this. My host took me in his arms and thanked me again and again. Then he looked at my *Philokalia,* saying, "I must certainly buy myself a copy of this. I will get it at once from Petersburg, but for the moment and in memory of this occasion, I will copy out the passage you have just read— you read it out to me." And then and there he wrote it out beautifully.

Then he exclaimed, "Why, goodness me! Of course I have an icon of the Damascene!" (It was probably of Saint John Damascene.) He picked up a frame, put what he had written behind the glass, and hung it beneath the icon. "There," said he, "the living word of the saint underneath his picture will often remind me to put his wholesome advice into practice."

After this we went to supper. As before, the whole household, men and women, sat down to table with us. How reverently silent and calm the meal was! And at the end of it, we all—the children as well—spent a long while in prayer. I was asked to read the "Akathist to Jesus the Heart's Delight." Afterwards, the servants went away to bed, and we three were left alone in the room. Then the lady brought me a white shirt and a pair of stockings. I bowed down at her feet, and said, "The stockings, little Mother, I will not take. I have never worn them in my life. We are always so used to *onoochi.*"[42] She hurried off and brought back her old caftan of thin yellow material, and cut it up into two *onoochi,* while her husband, saying, "And look, the poor fellow's footwear is almost worn out," brought me his new *bashmaki,*[43] large ones which he wore over his top boots.

Then he told me to go into the next room, which was empty, and change my shirt. I did so, and when I came back to them again they sat me down on a chair to put my new footwear on, he wrapping my feet and legs in the *onoochi* and she putting on the *bashmaki*. At first, I would not let them, but they bade me sit down, saying, "Sit down and be quiet. Christ washed his disciples' feet." There was nothing to do but obey, and I began to weep, and so did they. After this, the lady went to bed with the children, and her husband and I went to a summer house in the garden.

For a long while, we did not go to sleep, but lay talking. He began in this way: "Now in God's name and on your conscience, tell me the real truth. Who are you? You must be of good birth and are only assuming a disguise of simplicity. You read and write well; you speak correctly and are able to discuss things—and these things do not go with a peasant upbringing."

"I spoke the real truth with a sincere heart both to you and to your wife when I told you about my birth, and I never had a thought of lying or of deceiving you. Why should I? As for the things I say, they are not my own, but what I have heard from my departed *starets,* who was full of divine wisdom; or what I have gathered from a careful reading of the holy Fathers.

"But my ignorance has gained more light from interior prayer than from anything else, and that I have not reached by myself. It has been granted me by the mercy of God and the teaching of my *starets*. And that can be done by anyone. It costs nothing but the effort to sink down in silence into the depths of one's heart and call more and more upon the radiant name of Jesus. Everyone who does that feels at once the inward light. Everything becomes understandable to him; he even catches sight in this light of some of the mysteries of the kingdom of God. And what depth and light there is in the mystery of a man coming to know that he has this power to plumb the depths of his own being, to see himself from within, to find delight in self-knowledge, to take pity on himself and shed tears of gladness over his fall and his spoiled will! To show good sense in dealing with things and to talk with people is no hard matter, and lies within anyone's power—for the mind and the heart were there before learning and human wisdom. If the mind is there, you can set it to work either upon science or upon experience, but if the mind is lacking then no teaching, however wise, and no training will be any good. The trouble is that we live far from ourselves and have but little wish to get any nearer to ourselves. Indeed, we are running away all the time to avoid coming face to face with our real selves, and we barter the truth for trifles. We think, 'I would very gladly take an interest in spiritual things and in prayer, but I have no time. The fuss and cares of life give no chance for such a thing.' Yet, which is really important and necessary, salvation and the eternal life of the soul, or the fleeting life of the body on which we spend so much labor? It is that that I spoke of, and that leads to either sense or stupidity in people."

"Forgive me, dear Brother, I asked not just out of mere curiosity, but from friendliness and Christian sympathy, and even more because about two years ago I came across a case which gave rise to the question I put to you. It was like this: There came to our house a certain beggar with a discharged soldier's passport. He was old and feeble and so poor that he was almost naked and barefoot. He spoke little and in such a simple way that you would take him for a peasant of the steppes. We took him into the guest house, but some five days later he fell seriously ill, and so we moved him to this very summer house, where we kept him quiet, and my wife and I looked after him and nursed him. But after a while, it was plain that he was nearing his end.

"We prepared him for it and sent for our priest for his Confession, Communion, and Anointing. The day before he died, he got up and asked me for a sheet of paper and a pen, and begged me to shut the door and to let no one in while he wrote his will, which he desired me to send after his death to his son at an address in Petersburg. I was astounded when I saw him write, for not only did he write a beautiful and absolutely cultured hand, but the composition also was excellent, thoroughly correct, and showing great delicacy of touch. In fact, I'll read you that will of his tomorrow. I have a copy of it. All this set me wondering and aroused my curiosity enough to ask him about his origin and his life.

"After making me solemnly vow not to reveal it to anyone until after his death, he told me, for the glory of God, the story of his life. 'I was Prince X———,' he began. 'I was very wealthy and led a most luxurious and dissipated life. After the death of my wife, my son and I lived together, he being happily settled in military service; he was a captain in the Guards. One day when I was getting ready to go to a ball at an important person's house, I was very angry with my valet. Unable to control my temper, I struck him a severe blow on the head and ordered him to be sent away to his village. This happened in the evening, and next morning the valet died from the effects of the blow. This did not affect me very seriously. I regretted my rashness, but soon forgot the whole thing.

"'Six weeks later, though, I began seeing the dead valet; in my dreams to begin with; every night he disturbed me and reproached me, incessantly repeating, "Conscienceless man! You are my murderer!" As time went on, I began seeing him when I was awake also, wide awake. His appearances grew more and more frequent with the lapse of time, until the agitation he caused me became almost constant. And in the end, he did not appear alone, but I saw at the same time other dead men whom I had treated very badly, and women whom I had seduced. They all reproached me ceaselessly and gave me no peace, to such an extent that I could neither sleep nor eat nor do anything else.

"'My strength grew utterly exhausted and my skin stuck to my bones. All the efforts of skilled physicians were of no avail at all. I went abroad for a cure, but after trying it for six months, I was not benefited in the slightest degree, and those torturing apparitions grew steadily worse and worse. I was brought home again, more dead than alive. I went through the horrors and tortures of hell in fullest measure. I had proof then that hell exists, and I knew what it meant!

"'While I was in this wretched condition, I recognized my own wrongdoing. I repented and made my confession. I gave all my serfs their freedom and took a vow to afflict myself for the rest of my days with as toilsome a life as possible, and to disguise myself as a beggar. I wanted, because of all my sins, to become the humblest servant of people of the very lowest station in life.

"'No sooner had I resolutely come to this decision than those disturbing visions of mine ceased. I felt such comfort and happiness from having made my peace with God that I cannot adequately describe it. But just as I had been through hell before, so now I experienced paradise, and learned what that meant also, and how the kingdom of God is revealed in our hearts. I soon got perfectly well again and carried out my intention, leaving my native land secretly, furnished with a discharged soldier's passport.

"'And now for the last fifteen years I have been wandering about the whole of Siberia. Sometimes I hire myself out to the peasants for such work as I can do. Sometimes I find sustenance by begging in the name of Christ. Ah, what blessedness and what happiness and what peace of mind I enjoy in the midst of all these privations! It can be felt to the full only by one who, by the mercy of the Great Intercessor, has been brought out of hell into paradise.'

"When he came to the end of his story, he handed me the will to forward to his son and, on the following day, he died. And I have a copy of that will in a wallet lying on my Bible. If you would like to read it I will get it for you now.... Here you are."

I unfolded it and read thus: "In the name of God the glorious Trinity, the Father, the Son, and the Holy Ghost. My dearest Son, it is fifteen years now since you saw your father. But though you have had no news of him, he has, from time to time, found means to hear of you and cherished a father's love for you. That love impels him to send you these few lines from his deathbed. May they be a life-long lesson to you!

"You know how I suffered for my careless and thoughtless life. But you do not know how I have been blessed in my unknown pilgrimage and filled with joy in the fruits of repentance.

"I die at peace in the house of one who has been good to me, and to you also; for kindnesses showered upon the father must touch the feeling heart of a grateful son. Render to him my gratitude in any way you can.

"In bestowing on you my paternal blessing, I adjure you to remember God and to guard your conscience. Be prudent, kindly, and considerate; treat your inferiors as benevolently and amiably as you can; do not despise beggars and pilgrims, remembering that only in beggary and pilgrimage did your dying father find rest and peace for his tormented soul. I invoke God's blessing upon you and calmly close my eyes in the hope of life eternal, through the mercy of the Great Intercessor for men, our Lord Jesus Christ. Your father, X———."

Thus my host and I lay and chatted together and, in my turn, I put a question to him. "I suppose you are not without worries and bothers, with this guest house of yours? Of course there are quite a lot of our pilgrim brotherhood who take to the life because they have nothing to do, or from sheer laziness, and sometimes they do a little thieving on the road; I have seen it myself."

"There have not been many cases of that sort," was the answer. "We have, for the most part, always come across genuine pilgrims. And if we do get the other sort, we welcome them all the more kindly and try the harder to get them to stay with us. Through living with our good beggars and brothers in Christ, they often become reformed characters and leave the guest house humble and kindly folk. Why, there was a case of that sort not so long ago. He was a man belonging to the lower middle class of our town here, and he went so thoroughly to the bad that it came to the point of everybody driving him away from their doors with a stick and refusing to give him even a crust of bread. He was a drunken, quarrelsome bully and, what is more, he stole.

"That was the sort of person he was when, one day, he came to us very hungry and asked for some bread and wine, for the latter of which he was extraordinarily eager. We gave him a friendly reception and said, 'Stay with us and we will give you as much wine as you like, but only on this condition, that when you have been drinking, you go straight away and lie down and go to sleep. If you get in the slightest degree unruly or troublesome, not only shall we turn you out and never take you back again, but I shall report the matter to the police and have you sent off to a penal settlement as a suspected vagabond.'

"He agreed to this and stopped with us. For a week or more, he certainly did drink a great deal, to his heart's content. But because of his promise and because of his attachment to the wine, which he was afraid of being deprived of, he always lay down to sleep afterwards, or took himself off to the kitchen garden and lay down there quietly enough. When he was sober again, the brothers of the guest house talked persuasively to him and gave him good advice about learning to control himself, if only little by little to begin with. So he gradually began to drink less and, in the end, some three months later, he became quite a temperate person. He has taken a situation somewhere now and no longer leads a futile life of dependence on other people's charity. The day before yesterday he came here to thank me."

What wisdom, I thought, made perfect by the guidance of love! And aloud I said, "Blessed be God, who has so shown his grace in the household under your care." After this talk, we slept for an hour or an hour and a half, until we heard the bells of matins. We got ready and went over to the church. On going in, we at once saw the lady of the house, who had been there some time already with her children. We were all present at matins, and the divine liturgy went straight on afterwards. The head of the house, with his little boy, and I took our places within the altar,[44] while his wife and the little girl stood near the altar window, where they could see the elevation of the holy gifts. How earnestly they prayed as they knelt and shed tears of joy! And I wept to the full myself, as I looked at the light on their faces.

After the service was over, the gentlefolk, the priest, the servants, and the beggars all went off together to the dining room. There were some forty or so beggars and cripples and sick folk and children. They all sat down at one and the same table, and how peaceful and silent it all was. I plucked up my courage and said quietly to my host, "They read the lives of the saints during meals in monasteries. You might do the same. You've got the whole series of books."

"Let us adopt the plan here, Mary," said he, turning to his wife. "It will be most edifying. I will begin, and read at the first dinnertime, then you at the next, then the *batyushka*[45] and, after that, the rest of the brothers who know how to read, in turn."

The priest began to talk and eat at the same time. "I like listening, but as for reading—well, with all respect, I should like to be let off. You have no idea what a whirl I live in when I get home, worries and jobs of all sorts, first one thing has to be done and then another. What with a host of children and animals into the bargain, my whole day is filled up with things to do. There's no time for reading or study. I've long ago forgotten even what I learned at the seminary." I shuddered as I heard this, but our hostess, who was sitting near me, took my hand and said, *"Batyushka* talks like that because he is so humble. He always makes little of himself, but he is really a man of most kindly and saintly life. He has been a widower for the last twenty years and is bringing up a whole family of grandchildren. For all that, he holds services very frequently." At these words there came into my mind the following saying of Nicetas Stethatos in *The Philokalia:* "The nature of things is judged by the inward disposition of the soul," that is, a man gets his ideas about his neighbors from what he himself is. And he goes on to say, "He who has attained to true prayer and love has no sense of the differences between things. He does not distinguish the righteous man from the sinner, but loves them all equally and judges no man, as God causes his sun to shine and his rain to fall on the just and the unjust."

We fell silent again. Opposite me sat one of the beggars from the guest house who was quite blind. The master of the house was looking after him. He cut up his fish for him, gave him his spoon, and poured out his soup.

I watched carefully and saw that this beggar always had his mouth open and that his tongue was moving all the time, as though it were trembling. Surely, thought I, he must be one of those who prays—and I went on watching.

Right at the end of dinner, an old woman was taken ill. It was a sharp attack, and she began to groan. Our host and his wife took her into their bedroom and laid her on their bed, where the lady stayed to look after her. Her husband, meanwhile, ordered his carriage and went off at a gallop to the town for a doctor. The priest went to fetch the Holy Eucharist, and we all went our ways.

I felt, as it were, hungry for prayer, an urgent need to pour out my soul in prayer, and I had not been in quiet nor alone for forty-eight hours. I felt as though there were in my heart a sort of flood struggling to burst out and flow through all my limbs. To hold it back caused me severe, even if comforting, pain in the heart—a pain which needed to be calmed and satisfied in the silence of prayer. And now I saw why those who really practice interior self-acting prayer have fled from the company of men and hidden themselves in unknown places. I saw further why the venerable Isaac called even the most spiritual and helpful talk mere idle chatter if there were too much of it, just as Ephrem the Syrian says, "Good speech is silver, but silence is pure gold."

As I thought all this over, I made my way to the guest house, where everyone was resting after dinner. I went up into the attic, where I quietly rested and prayed. When the beggars were about again, I found the blind man and took him off to the kitchen garden, where we sat down alone and began to talk. "Tell me, please," said I, "do you for the sake of your soul say the Prayer of Jesus?"

"I have said it without stopping for a long while."

"But what sort of feeling do you get from it?"

"Only this, that day or night I cannot live without the Prayer."

"How did God show it you? Tell me about it, tell me everything, dear Brother."

"Well, it was like this. I belong to this district and used to earn my living by doing tailoring jobs. I traveled about different provinces going from village to village, and made clothes for the peasants. I happened to stay a fairly long time in one village in the house of a peasant for whose family I was making clothing. One day, a holy day it was, I saw three books lying near the icons, and I asked who it was in the household that could read. 'No one,' they answered. 'Those books were left us by an uncle. He knew how to read and write.' I picked up one of the books, opened it at random, and read, as I remember to this very hour, the following words, 'Ceaseless prayer is to call upon the name of God always. Whether a man is conversing or sitting down or walking or making something or eating—whatever he may be doing—in all places and at all times, he ought to call upon God's name.'

"Reading that started me thinking—how simple that would be for me. I began to say prayer in a whisper while I was sewing, and I liked it. People living in the same house with me noticed it and began to make fun of me. 'Are you a wizard or what,' they asked, 'going on whispering all the time?' Or 'What are you muttering charms about?' So to hide what I was doing, I gave up moving my lips and went on saying the Prayer with my tongue only. In the end, I got so used to the Prayer that my tongue went on saying it by itself day and night, and I liked it.

"I went about like that for a long while, and then all of a sudden I became quite blind. Almost everyone in our family gets 'dark water'[46] in the eyes. So, because I was so poor, our people got me into the alms house at Tobolsk, which is the capital of our province.

I am on my way there now, only these good people have kept me here because they want to give me a cart as far as Tobolsk."

"What was the name of the book you read? Wasn't it called *The Philokalia*?"

"Honestly, I don't know. I didn't even look at the title page."

I fetched my *Philokalia* and searched out those very words of the Patriarch Callistus, which he had said by heart, and I read them to him.

"Why, those are the very same words!" cried the blind man. "How splendid! Go on reading, Brother."

When I got to the lines, "One ought to pray with the heart," he began to ply me with questions. "What does that mean? How is that done?"

I told him that full teaching on praying with the heart was given in this same book, *The Philokalia*. He begged me eagerly to read the whole thing to him.

"This is what we will do," said I. "When are you starting for Tobolsk?"

"Straight away," he answered.

"Very well then. I am also going to take the road again tomorrow. We will go together, and I will read it all to you—all about praying with the heart. And I will show you how to find where your heart is and to enter it."

"And what about the cart?" he asked.

"What does the cart matter? We know how far it is to Tobolsk— a mere hundred miles. We will take it easy, and think how nice it will be going along, just we two together alone, talking and reading about the Prayer as we go." And so it was agreed.

In the evening, our host came himself to call us all to supper and, after the meal, we told him that the blind man and I were taking the road together, and that we did not need a cart, so as to be able to read *The Philokalia* more easily. Hearing this he said, "I also liked *The Philokalia* very much, and I have already written a letter and got the money ready to send to Petersburg when

I go into court tomorrow, so as to get a copy sent me by return of post."

So we set off on our way next morning, after thanking them very warmly for their great love and kindness. Both of them came with us for more than half a mile from their house. And so we bade each other goodbye.

We went on, the blind man and I, by easy stages, doing from six to ten miles a day. All the rest of the time we spent sitting down in lonely places and reading *The Philokalia*. I read him the whole part about praying with the heart, in the order which my departed *starets* had shown me, that is, beginning with the writings of Nicephorus the Monk, Gregory of Sinai, and so on. How eagerly and closely he listened to it all, and what happiness and joy it brought him!

Then he began to put such questions to me about prayer as my mind was not equal to finding answers to. When we had read what we needed from *The Philokalia,* he eagerly begged me actually to show him the way the mind finds the heart, how to bring the divine name of Jesus Christ into it, and how to find the joy of praying inwardly with the heart. And I told him all about it thus: "Now you, as a blind man, can see nothing. Yet, as a matter of fact, you can imagine with your mind and picture to yourself what you have seen in time past, such as a man or some object or other, or one of your own limbs. For instance, can you not picture your hand or your foot as clearly as if you were looking at it? Can you not turn your eyes to it and fix them upon it, blind as they are?"

"Yes, I can," he answered.

"Then picture to yourself your heart in just the same way. Turn your eyes to it just as though you were looking at it through your breast, and picture it as clearly as you can. And with your ears, listen closely to its beating, beat by beat. When you have got into the way of doing this, begin to fit the words of the Prayer to the beats of the heart, one after the other, looking at it all the time. Thus, with the first beat, say or think *'Lord,'* with the second, *'Jesus,'* with the third, *'Christ,'* with the fourth, *'have mercy,'* and with the fifth, *'on me.'* And do it over and over again. This will come easily to you, for you already know the groundwork and the first part of praying with the heart.

"Afterwards, when you have grown used to what I have just told you about, you must begin bringing the whole Prayer of Jesus into and out of your heart in time with your breathing, as the Fathers taught. Thus, as you draw your breath in, say or imagine yourself saying, *'Lord Jesus Christ,'* and as you breathe out again, *'have mercy on me.'* Do this as often and as much as you can and, in a short space of time, you will feel a slight and not unpleasant pain in your heart, followed by a warmth. Thus by God's help, you will get the joy of self-acting inward prayer of the heart. But then, whatever you do, be on your guard against imagination and any sort of visions. Don't accept any of them whatever, for the holy Fathers lay down most strongly that inward prayer should be kept free from visions, lest one fall into temptation."

The blind man listened closely to all this and began eagerly to do with his heart what I had shown him, and he spent a long while at it, especially during the nighttime at our halting places. In about five days' time, he began to feel the warmth very much, as well as a happiness beyond words in his heart, and a great wish to devote himself unceasingly to this prayer which stirred up in him a love of Jesus Christ. From time to time, he saw a light, though he could make out no objects in it. And sometimes, when he made the entrance into his heart, it seemed to him as though a flame, as of a lighted candle, blazed up strongly and happily in his heart and, rushing outwards through his throat, flooded him with light. And in the light of this flame he could see even far-off things, and this did indeed happen once. We were walking through a forest, and he was silent, wholly given up to the Prayer. Suddenly he said to me, "What a pity! The church is already on fire. There, the belfry has fallen."

"Stop this vain dreaming," I answered. "It is a temptation to you. You must put all such fancies aside at once. How can you possibly see what is happening in the town? We are still seven or eight miles away from it."

He obeyed me and went on with his prayer in silence. Toward evening, we came to the town and there, as a matter of fact, I saw several burnt houses and a fallen belfry, which had been built with ties of timber, and people crowding around and wondering how it was that the belfry had crushed no one in its fall. As I worked it out, the misfortune had happened at the very same time as the blind man spoke to me about it. And he began to talk to me on the matter. "You told me," said he, "that this vision of mine was vain, but here you see things really are as I saw them. How can I fail to thank and to love the Lord Jesus Christ, who shows his grace even to sinners and the blind and the foolish! And I thank you also for teaching me the work of the heart."

"Love Jesus Christ," said I, "and thank him all you will. But beware of taking your visions for direct revelations of grace. For these things may often happen quite naturally in the order of things. The human soul is not bound by place and matter. It can see even in the darkness and what happens a long way off, as well as things near at hand. Only, we do not give force and scope to this spiritual power. We crush it beneath the yoke of our gross bodies or get it mixed up with our haphazard thoughts and ideas. But when we concentrate within ourselves, when we draw away from everything around us and become more subtle and refined in mind, then the soul comes into its own and works to its fullest power.

"So what happened was natural enough. I have heard my departed *starets* say that there are people (even such as are not given to prayer, but who have this sort of power, or gain it during sickness), who see light even in the darkest of rooms, as though it streamed from every article in it, and see things by it; who see their doubles and enter into the thoughts of other people. But what does come direct from the grace of God in the case of the prayer of the heart is so full of sweetness and delight that no tongue can tell of it, nor can it be likened to anything material; it is beyond compare. No feeling can be compared to the sweet knowledge of grace in the heart."

My blind friend listened eagerly to this and became still more humble. The Prayer grew more and more in his heart, and delighted him beyond words. I rejoiced at this with all my soul and thanked God from my heart that he had let me see so blessed a servant of His. We got to Tobolsk at last. I took him to the alms house and, leaving him there with a loving farewell, I went on my own way.

I went along without hurrying for about a month with a deep sense of the way in which good lives teach us and spur us on to copy them. I read *The Philokalia* a great deal, and there made sure of everything I had told the blind man of prayer. His example kindled in me zeal and thankfulness and love for God. The prayer of my heart gave me such consolation that I felt there was no happier person on earth than I, and I doubted if there could be greater and fuller happiness in the kingdom of heaven. Not only did I feel this in my own soul, but the whole outside world also seemed to me full of charm and delight. Everything drew me to love and to thank God: people, trees, plants, animals. I saw them all as my kinsfolk. I found on all of them the magic of the name of Jesus. Sometimes I felt as light as though I had no body and was floating happily through the air instead of walking. Sometimes when I withdrew into myself, I saw clearly all my internal organs and was filled with wonder at the wisdom with which the human body is made. Sometimes I felt as joyful as if I had been made a tsar. And at all such times of happiness, I wished that God would let death come to me quickly and let me pour out my heart in thankfulness at his feet in the world of spirits.

It would seem that somehow I took too great a joy in these feelings, or perhaps it was just allowed by God's will, but for some time I felt a sort of quaking and fear in my heart. Was there, I wondered, some new misfortune or trouble coming upon me like what happened after I met the girl again to whom I taught the Prayer of Jesus in the chapel? A cloud of such thoughts came down upon me, and I remembered the words of the venerable John Karpathisky, who says that "The master will often submit to humiliation and endure disaster and temptation for the sake of those who have profited by him spiritually." I fought against the gloomy thoughts and prayed with more earnestness than ever. The Prayer put them to flight and, taking heart again, I said, "God's will be done. I am ready to suffer whatever Jesus Christ sends me for my wickedness and pride. And those to whom I had lately shown the secret of entry into the heart and interior prayer had, even before their meeting with me, been made ready by the direct and secret teaching of God." Calmed by these thoughts, I went on my way again filled with consolation, having the Prayer with me and happier even than I had been before.

It rained for a couple of days, and the road was so muddy that I could hardly drag my feet out of the mire. I was walking across the steppe and, in ten miles or so, I did not find a single dwelling. At last, toward nightfall, I came upon one house standing by itself right on the road. Glad I was to see it and I thought I would ask for a rest and a night's lodging here and see what God sent for the morrow; perhaps the weather would get better. As I drew near, I saw a tipsy old man in a soldier's cloak sitting on the *zavalina*. I greeted him, saying, "Could I perhaps ask someone to give me a night's lodging here?"

"Who else could give it you but me?" he shouted. "I'm master here. This is a posting station and I am in charge of it."

"Then will you allow me, sir, to spend the night at your house?"

"Have you got a passport? Give some legal account of yourself."

I handed him my passport and, holding it in his hands, he again asked, "Where is your passport?"

"You have it in your hands," I answered.

"Well, come into the house," said he.

He put his spectacles on, read the passport through, and said, "All right, that's all in order. Stay the night. I'm a good fellow really. Have a drink."

"I don't drink," I answered, "and never have."

"Well, please yourself, I don't care. At any rate, have supper with us."

They sat down to table, he and the cook—a young woman who also had been drinking rather freely—and asked me to sit down with them. They quarreled all through supper, hurling reproaches at each other and, in the end, came to blows. The man went off into the passage and to his bed in a lumber room, while the cook began to tidy up and wash up the cups and spoons, all the while going on with the abuse of her master. I took a seat, thinking it would be some time before she quieted down.

So I asked her where I could sleep, for I was very tired from my journey. "I will make you up a bed," she answered. And she placed another bench against the one under the front window, spread a felt blanket over them, and gave me a pillow. I lay down and shut my eyes as though asleep. For a long while yet the cook bustled about, but at last she tidied up, put out the fire, and was coming over toward me.

Suddenly the whole window, which was in a corner at the front of the house—frame, glass, and splinters of wood—flew into shivers which came showering down with a frightful crash. The whole house shook and from outside the window came a sickening groan and shouts and the noise of struggling. The woman sprang back in terror into the middle of the room and fell in a heap on the floor. I jumped up with my wits all astray, thinking the earth had opened under my feet. And the next thing is I see two drivers carrying a man into the house so covered with blood that you could not even see his face. And this added still more to my horror. He was a king's messenger who had galloped here to change horses. His driver had not taken the turn into the gateway properly, the carriage pole knocked out the window and, as there was a ditch in front of the house, the carriage overturned and the king's messenger was thrown out, cutting his head badly on a sharp post.

He asked for some water and wine to bathe his wound. Then he drank a glass and cried, "Horses!"

I went up to him and said, "Surely, sir, you won't travel any further with a wound like that."

"A king's messenger has no time to be ill," he answered, and galloped off.

The drivers dragged the senseless woman into a corner near the stove and covered her with a rug, saying, "She was badly scared. She'll come round all right." The master of the house had another glass and went back to bed, and I was left alone.

Very soon the woman got up again and began walking across the room from corner to corner in a witless sort of way and, in the end, she went out of the house. I felt as though the shock had taken all the strength out of me and, after saying my prayers, I dropped asleep for a while before dawn.

In the morning I took leave of the old man and set off again and, as I walked, I sent up my prayer with faith and trust and thanks to the Father of all blessing and consolation who had saved me when I was in such great danger.

Some six years after this happened, I was passing a convent and went into the church to pray. The kindly abbess welcomed me in her room after the liturgy and had tea served. Suddenly some unexpected guests came to see her and she went to them, leaving me with some of the nuns who waited on her in her cell. One of them, who was pouring out tea and was clearly a humble soul, made me curious enough to ask whether she had been in the convent long.

"Five years," she answered. "I was out of my mind when they brought me here, and it was here that God had mercy on me. The mother abbess kept me to wait on her in her cell and led me to take the veil."

"How came you to go out of your mind?" I asked.

"It was fright," said she. "I used to work at a posting station and, late one night, some horses knocked in a window. I was so terrified that it drove me out of my mind. For a whole year my relations took me from one shrine to another, but it was only here that I got cured." When I heard this I rejoiced in spirit and praised God who so wisely orders all things for the best.

"I had a great many other experiences," I said, speaking to my spiritual father, "but I should want three whole days and nights to tell you everything as it happened. Still there is one other thing I will tell you about."

One clear summer's day I noticed a cemetery near the road, and what they call a *pogost,* that is, a church with some houses for those who minister in it. The bells were ringing for the liturgy, and I made my way toward it. People who lived round about were going the same way, and some of them, before they got as far as the church, were sitting on the grass. Seeing me hurrying along, they said to me, "Don't hurry, you'll have plenty of time for standing about when the service begins. Services take a very long while here: our priest is in bad health and goes very slowly."

The service did, in fact, last a very long while. The priest was a young man, but very thin and pale. He celebrated very slowly indeed, but with great devotion and, at the end of the liturgy, he preached with much feeling a beautiful and simple sermon on how to grow in love for God. The priest asked me into his house and to stay to dinner.

During the meal I said, "How reverently and slowly you celebrate, Father!"

"Yes," he answered, "but my parishioners do not like it and they grumble. Still, there's nothing to be done about it. I like to meditate on each prayer and rejoice in it before I say it aloud. Without that interior appreciation and feeling, every word uttered is useless both to myself and to others. Everything centers in the interior life and in attentive prayer! Yet how few concern themselves with the interior life," he went on. "It is because they feel no desire to cherish the spiritual inward light."

"And how is one to reach that?" I asked. "It would seem to be very difficult."

"Not at all," was the reply. "To attain spiritual enlightenment and become a man of recollected interior life, you should take one or the other of holy Scripture and, for as long a period as possible, concentrate on that alone all your power of attention and meditation; then the light of understanding will be revealed to you. You must proceed in the same way about prayer. If you want it to be pure, right, and enjoyable, you must choose some short prayer, consisting of few but forcible words, and repeat it frequently and for a long while. Then you will find delight in prayer."

This teaching of the priest pleased me very much. How practical and simple it was and yet, at the same time, how deep and how wise. I gave thanks to God in my thoughts for showing me such a true pastor of his church.

When the meal was over, he said to me, "You have a sleep after dinner while I read the Bible and prepare my sermon for tomorrow." So I went into the kitchen. There was no one there except a very old woman sitting crouched in a corner, coughing. I sat down under a small window, took *The Philokalia* out of my knapsack, and began to read quietly to myself. After a while I heard the old woman who was sitting in the corner ceaselessly whispering the Prayer of Jesus. It gave me great joy to hear the Lord's most holy name spoken so often, and I said to her, "What a good thing it is, Mother, that you are always saying the Prayer. It is a most Christian and most wholesome action."

"Yes," she replied. "The 'Lord have mercy' is the only thing I have to lean on in my old age."

"Have you made a habit of this prayer for long?"

"Since I was quite young, yes, and I couldn't live without it, for the Jesus Prayer saved me from ruin and death."

"How? Please tell me about it, for the glory of God and in praise of the blessed power of the Prayer of Jesus."

I put *The Philokalia* away in my knapsack and took a seat nearer to her, and she began her story.

"I used to be a young and pretty girl. My parents gave me in marriage and, the very day before the wedding, my bridegroom came to see us. Suddenly, before he had taken a dozen steps, he dropped down and died without a single gasp. This frightened me so that I utterly refused to marry at all. I made up my mind to live unmarried, to go on pilgrimages to the shrines, and pray at them. However, I was afraid to travel all by myself, young as I was. I feared evil people might molest me. But an old woman-pilgrim whom I knew taught me wherever my road took me always to say the Jesus Prayer without stopping, and told me for certain that if I did, no misfortune of any sort could happen to me on my way. I proved the truth of this, for I walked even to far-off shrines and never came to any harm. My parents gave me the money for my journeys. As I grew old I lost my health and now the priest here, out of the kindness of his heart, gives me board and lodging."

I was overjoyed to hear this and knew not how to thank God for this day in which I had been taught so much by examples of spiritual life. Then, asking the kindly and devout priest for his blessing, I set off again on my way, rejoicing.

Then again, not so long ago, as I was making my way here through the Kazan province, I had a chance of learning how the power of prayer in the name of Jesus Christ is shown clearly and strongly even in those who use it without a will to do so, and how saying the Prayer often and for a long time is a sure and rapid way to gaining its blessed fruits. It happened that I was to pass the night at a Tartar village. On reaching it I saw a Russian carriage and coachman outside the window of one of the huts. The horses were being fed nearby. I was glad to see all this and made up my mind to ask for a night's lodging at the same place, thinking that I should at least spend the night with Christians.[47]

When I came up to them I asked the coachman where he was going, and he answered that his master was going from Kazan to the Crimea. While I was talking with the coachman, his master pulled open the carriage curtains from inside, looked out, and saw me. Then he said, "I shall stay the night here, too, but I have not gone into the hut; Tartar houses are so uncomfortable. I have decided to spend the night in the carriage." Then he got out and, as it was a fine evening, we strolled about for a while and talked. He asked me a lot of questions and talked about himself also, and this is what he told me.

"Until I was sixty-five I was a captain in the navy but, as I grew old, I became the victim of gout—an incurable disease. So I retired from the service and lived, almost constantly ill, on a farm of my wife's in the Crimea. She was an impulsive woman of a volatile disposition, and a great card player. She found it boring living with a sick man and left me, going off to our daughter in Kazan, who happened to be married to a civil servant there. My wife laid hands on all she could, and even took the servants with her, leaving me with nobody but an eight-year-old boy, my godson. So I lived alone for about three years.

"The boy who served me was a sharp little fellow and capable of doing all the household work. He did my room, heated the stove, cooked the gruel, and got the samovar[48] ready. But at the same time he was extraordinarily mischievous and full of spirits. He was incessantly rushing about and banging and shouting and playing and up to all sorts of tricks, so that he disturbed me exceedingly. And I, being ill and bored, liked to read spiritual books all the time. I had one splendid book by Gregory Palamas, on the Prayer of Jesus. I read it almost continuously, and I used to say the Prayer to some extent. But the boy hindered me, and no threats and no punishment restrained him from indulging in his pranks.

"At last I hit upon the following method. I made him sit on a bench in my room with me and bade him say the Prayer of Jesus without stopping. At first this was extraordinarily distasteful to him, and he tried all sorts of ways to avoid it, and often fell silent. In order to make him do my bidding, I kept a cane beside me. When he said the Prayer, I quietly read my book or listened to how he was saying it. But let him stop for a moment, and I showed him the cane, then he got frightened and took to the Prayer again. I found this very peaceful, and quiet reigned in the house.

"After a while I noticed that now there was no need of the cane; the boy began to do my bidding quite willingly and eagerly. Further, I observed a complete change in his mischievous character. He became quiet and taciturn and performed his household tasks better than before. I was glad of this and began to allow him more freedom. And what was the result? Well, in the end, he got so accustomed to the Prayer that he was saying it almost the whole time, whatever he was doing and without any compulsion from me at all. When I asked him about it, he answered that he felt an insuperable desire to be saying the Prayer always. 'And what are your feelings while doing so?' I asked him.

"'Nothing,' said he, 'only I feel that it's nice to be saying it.'

"'How do you mean—nice?'

"'I don't know how to put it exactly.'

"'Makes you feel cheerful, do you mean?'

"'Yes, cheerful.'

"He was twelve years old when the Crimean War broke out, and I went to stay with my daughter at Kazan, taking him with me. Here he lived in the kitchen with the other servants, and this bored him very much. He would come to me with complaints that the others, playing and joking among themselves, bothered him also, and laughed at him and so prevented him saying his Prayer. In the end, after about three months, he came to me and said, 'I am going home. I'm unbearably sick of this place and all this noise.'

"'How can you go alone for such a distance and in winter, too?' said I. 'Wait, and when I go I'll take you with me.' Next day my boy had vanished.

"We sent everywhere to look for him but nowhere could he be found. In the end I got a letter from the Crimea, from the people who were on our farm, saying that the boy had been found dead in my empty house on the April 4, which was Easter Monday. He was lying peacefully on the floor of my room with his hands folded on his breast and, in that same thin frock coat that he always went about my house in, and which he was wearing when he went away. And so they buried him in my garden.

"When I heard this news I was absolutely amazed. How had the child reached the farm so quickly? He started on February 26, and he was found on April 4. Even with God's help, you want horses to cover 2,000 miles in a month! Why, it is nearly seventy miles a day! And in thin clothes, without a passport, and without a farthing in his pocket into the bargain! Even supposing that someone may have given him a lift on the way, still that in itself would be a mark of God's special providence and care for him. That boy of mine, mark you, enjoyed the fruits of prayer," concluded this gentleman, "and here am I, an old man, still not as far on as he."

Later on I said to him, "It is a splendid book, sir, the one by Gregory Palamas, which you said you liked reading. I know it. But it treats rather of the oral Prayer of Jesus. You should read a book called *The Philokalia.* There you will find a full and complete study of how to reach the spiritual Prayer of Jesus in the mind and heart also, and taste the sweet fruit of it." At the same time I showed him my *Philokalia* I saw that he was pleased to have this advice of mine, and he promised that he would get a copy for himself.

And in my own mind I dwelt upon the wonderful ways in which the power of God is shown in this Prayer. What wisdom and teaching there was in the story I had just heard! The cane taught the Prayer to the boy and, what is more, as a means of consolation, it became a help to him. Are not our own sorrows and trials which we meet with on the road of prayer in the same way the rod in God's hand? Why, then, are we so frightened and troubled when our heavenly Father in the fullness of his boundless love lets us see them, and when these rods teach us to be more earnest in learning to pray and lead us on to consolation which is beyond words?

When I came to the end of the things I had to tell, I said to my spiritual father: "Forgive me, in God's name. I have already chattered far too much. And the holy Fathers call even spiritual talk mere babble if it lasts too long. It is time I went to find my fellow traveler to Jerusalem. Pray for me, a miserable sinner, that of his great mercy, God may bless my journey."

"With all my heart I wish it, dear Brother in the Lord," he replied. "May the all-loving grace of God shed its light on your path and go with you, as the angel Raphael went with Tobias!"

Commentary IV

New Encounters on the Journey

"What unexpected things we meet with on life's journey!
Yet all the while, God and His holy providence guide our
actions and overrule our plans."

FROM THE WAY OF A PILGRIM

℘

I n the fourth narrative, the Pilgrim's plans undergo a slight change; he agrees to escort an elderly deaf man along the way by horse and wagon. Thus, rather than setting out on foot immediately for Odessa, the first leg of his journey to Jerusalem, the Pilgrim and the elderly man decide not to leave until the third day after Christmas. As a result of this delay, the Pilgrim is able to make a second visit to his spiritual father and to relate some of the educational experiences he has had in his life of wandering. The narrative includes the circumstances surrounding his delayed departure, his educational experiences in a provincial town with a pious family and a blind beggar, an incident in a post office and, finally, his departure for Jerusalem, which also serves as a conclusion for the entire book. Each of these episodes provides us with some important insights into both the prayer of the heart and spiritual direction.

THE PILGRIM'S DELAYED DEPARTURE

Summary

"The Russian proverb is true, which says that 'man proposes but God disposes.' "[49] With these words, the Pilgrim opens his second— and quite unexpected—visit with his spiritual father. He tells him that he seeks his advice on how to handle a totally unforeseen incident that has kept him in Irkutsk for three more days. He tells his spiritual father that he had gotten as far as the outskirts of the town, when he saw a man who was once a pilgrim like himself, a friend whom he hadn't seen for nearly three years. They talked for a while and, when it came out that the Pilgrim was heading for Jerusalem, the man told him that he had just the right traveling companion for him. The Pilgrim was hesitant at first, especially since he was not used to traveling with companions. When he heard the particulars of the story, however, he came to see the hand of God in this strange turn of events and tentatively agreed to the proposal.

As the story goes, the Pilgrim's friend works for a man whose father had also vowed to go on pilgrimage to Jerusalem. His family is reluctant to let him travel alone, however, because he is elderly and completely deaf. To make it easier for the man, his family is insisting that he travel by horse and wagon, and they are currently looking for someone they could trust to serve as his companion. The Pilgrim visits this family with his friend and, recognizing the family's genuine need, agrees to help them out by serving as the old man's escort to Odessa. They agree to leave on the third day after Christmas. With time on his hands before his departure, the Pilgrim is now in a position to tell his spiritual father about some of the educational experiences he has had on his lengthy pilgrimages.

Reflection

This opening scene brings three observations to mind. First, the Pilgrim's generosity and willingness to change one of his most in-grained habits of behavior (for example, traveling alone) is a reflection of his deep spiritual life. The interior prayer of the heart has a direct effect on a person's relationship with others. In this case, it makes the Pilgrim more sensitive to those in need and willing to sacrifice his own way of doing things in order to help others. That he recognizes the hand of God in an otherwise unwanted burden signals some of the progress he has made in the spiritual life.

Second, the Pilgrim, who states early on that he has come to his spiritual father for advice on how to handle the situation, has done the hard work of discerning almost entirely on his own. His spiritual father does nothing but listen to and then confirm what the Pilgrim has himself already decided. This is yet another indication that the Pilgrim's apprenticeship in unceasing prayer has borne fruit. It shows that he is growing less and less dependent on another's guidance in practical decisions, and that he is becoming more self-directed in his discernment in the implementation of the will of God for his life.

Finally, the Pilgrim's decision to set out on his journey with a traveling companion is a symbolic representation of the role he himself will increasingly take on as a spiritual guide. Although he himself is a self-directed individual, he decides to travel with someone who does not have the strength to make it alone. Since "faith comes through hearing" (Rom 10:17), the fact that his companion is deaf has deep spiritual import for the Pilgrim; he will help this man get closer to Jerusalem, the Holy City, hopefully mediating for him an even deeper experience of faith along the way.

These concrete circumstances of the Pilgrim's journey symbolize a change in his vocation. No longer is he simply a wandering traveler in search of the mysteries of unceasing prayer. Rather, having learned them himself from his departed *starets*, he now takes on the role of imparting them to others. When seen in this light, the rest of the experiences he recounts in the fourth narrative show how God has, all along, readied him for this fundamental change in calling.

THE PILGRIM LEARNS THROUGH EXPERIENCE

For most of the fourth narrative, the Pilgrim is concerned with relating some of his more impressionable educational experiences as
a pilgrim. These can be divided into five sections: (1) his experience in a provincial town; (2) his visit with a pious family; (3) his
encounter with a blind beggar; (4) his stay in a post office; and (5) his
account of two brief village experiences.

These sections are prefaced, however, by some interesting comments on the obstacles to prayer that the Pilgrim's late *starets* tells
him he would encounter in his journeys. These come from the left
and from the right. The former, which he terms as being theft from
the left-hand side, are temptations of vain thoughts and sinful
imaginings; the latter, which he terms as being theft from the right-
hand side, are memories of all sorts of pleasant thoughts and edifying things that would lure him away from prayer.[50] Both forms of
temptations are dangerous to one's spiritual life. He remembers his
starets telling him that to spend more of the day in edifying speculation or conversation than in the essential hidden prayer of the heart
was self-seeking spiritual gluttony. Beginners, especially, have to
be careful of giving in to such temptations. The time they spend in
prayer should far exceed all their other devotional activities.

In addition to this opening spiritual teaching about the obstacles
to prayer, the Pilgrim admits that so many things, both good and
bad, have happened to him that it would be impossible to recount
them all. What he does remember tends to be those things that have
helped him in his prayer. The rest he has not bothered with.

The Pilgrim's Experience in a Provincial Town: Summary
The first experience the Pilgrim shares with his spiritual father has
to do with his travels through the province of Tobolsk. He says that
he happens to be passing through one of the towns of that district
when he notices that he is running out of dried bread. When he
stops in at one of the houses to ask for food, the master and mistress

of the house give him not only a warm loaf of freshly baked bread, but a brand new knapsack as well. Later, as he is leaving the town, he stops in a small shop to ask for some salt and receives a small bag of it from the shopkeeper. He rejoices at his good fortune and thanks God for bringing such good people into his life since, on their account, he does not have to worry about food for a whole week.

Reflection

In this first experience, the Pilgrim shows how his belief in God's providential care manifests itself in the nitty-gritty details of his life. He looks for dried bread and receives not just a fresh loaf of bread, but a sturdy new knapsack as well. He asks for a little salt and receives a whole bag of it. Bread and salt, some of the essential ingredients of his diet, come to him in abundance. He leaves the town giving thanks to God not just for meeting his needs, but for far exceeding them. He is happy because he does not have to worry about where he is going to find his next meal, and he will be able to sleep better at night as a result. This experience of God's care echoes Jesus' words in the Gospel when he says: "It is not for you to be in search of what you are to eat or drink. Stop worrying. The unbelievers of this world are always running after these things. Your Father knows that you need such things. Seek out instead his kingship over you, and the rest will follow in turn" (Lk 12:29–31). Although the Pilgrim is not yet free of all worry about such things, he is far more advanced than most. These concrete experiences of human generosity confirm him in the path he has chosen and fill him with gratitude to God for taking such good care of him.

The Pilgrim Visits a Pious Family: Summary

The Pilgrim next tells his spiritual father about his stay with a devout Christian family. After walking about three and a half miles from the town, he comes across a poor village. As he approaches its small wooden church, two young and extremely well-dressed children call out to him and beg him to come home with them so that he can meet their mother. He does so willingly and is taken aback by the hospitality he receives. The children's mother extends such a warm welcome to the Pilgrim and insists that he stay with them until her husband arrives. He agrees to have dinner with them and is amazed to see the servants sit down and eat with them. When they take a stroll in the garden after eating, the mother tells him the story of her family.

Her mother, now a nun in a convent in Tobolsk, is the great-granddaughter of Saint Joasaph, whose relics are in Byelograd. Her husband, the son of a poor nobleman, is taken in by her family when he is orphaned as a child and is raised like a member of the family. When the two of them grow up, her mother signs her estate over to them and they marry. Before entering the convent, she gives her daughter and her son-in-law five instructions: (1) to live as good Christians; (2) to say their prayers fervently to God; (3) to love their neighbors and especially to feed the hungry; (4) to bring up their children in the fear of the Lord; and (5) to treat their serfs as brothers and sisters. She concludes her brief story by saying that she and her husband have been trying to live by these instructions for the last ten years. She tells him that they even have a special guest house for the poor where there are more than ten people residing at the present moment.

When the husband finally arrives, the Pilgrim receives an equally warm welcome. The man takes him into his study and shows him many of the fine books in his possession. Gradually, the topic turns to prayer and the master pulls out a commentary on the Our Father. When his wife comes in with tea and a large silver basket filled with pastries, he gives her the book and asks her to read from it. As she does, the Pilgrim has a deep experience of prayer, one in which he is able to listen to the what the woman is reading while attending to the prayer of his heart. It is then, too, that he feels as though the spirit of his *starets* has penetrated his own spirit and illuminated it.

When the wife finishes her reading, the Pilgrim, seeing that the commentary focuses primarily on Christian works, introduces the husband and wife to the mystical meaning of the Our Father as it appears in Maximus the Confessor, Peter the Damascene, and especially in *The Philokalia*. The master is especially taken by the Pilgrim's explanation and resolves to buy a copy of this holy book. In the meantime, he writes down one of the passages of Peter the Damascene that the Pilgrim recites and places it in the frame of a holy icon.

After this period of instruction, the master of the house and his wife fit the Pilgrim with an entirely new set of clothes. As they put new linen on his feet and fit him with new shoes, the Pilgrim remembers how Christ washed the feet of his disciples (see Jn 13:1–17) and is brought to tears.

After the rest of the household goes to bed, the master talks with the Pilgrim deep into the early morning hours and touches on such topics as the Pilgrim's true identity and how he deals with troublemakers in his guest house. Finally, after sleeping for about an hour and a half, they rise for matins and then the divine liturgy and return to the house for breakfast where everyone—the gentlefolk, the priest, the beggars, and the servants—are gathered for the meal. The Pilgrim suggests that they read from the lives of the saints, and the group is not only willing to comply, but even decide to do it on a regular basis. The priest, of all people, does not respond favorably to this suggestion, however, saying that he is so busy that he has no more time for reading. The Pilgrim shudders when he hears this, but the mistress of the house defends the priest, saying that he always humbles himself and is a righteous and kind man. This makes the Pilgrim think of the saying of Nicetas Stethatos in *The Philokalia*: "The nature of things is judged by the inward disposition of the soul, that is, a man gets his ideas about his neighbors from what he himself is."[51] It is during this same meal that the Pilgrim notices a blind beggar seated at table who is mysteriously moving his tongue. This encounter becomes the subject of the next story he recounts to his spiritual father.

Reflection

When looking at this second experience that the Pilgrim shares with his spiritual father, we are struck first by the basic goodness of these gentle Christian people. The master of the house and his wife treat the Pilgrim, a total stranger, as if he were a member of their own family, bringing to mind the words of Jesus to his disciples: "Be compassionate, as your Father in heaven is compassionate" (Lk 6:36). Nothing that they have in their possession is too good to share with him. He and a host of others partake of their generosity and kindness in an extraordinary way. Their gathering at table—family members, priest, Pilgrim, beggars, and servants—reminds one of the parable in which the king sends his servants into the byroads to round up everyone they meet in order to fill his banquet hall (see Mt 22:10). Through this kind Christian family, the Pilgrim experiences a foretaste of the heavenly banquet, were there does not exist "...Jew or Greek, slave or freeman, male or female" (Gal 3:28).

The Pilgrim, however, is not merely on the receiving end of the relationship. He is with them only a short time before he starts sharing with them the wealth of his firsthand knowledge on the prayer of the heart. He speaks of how his own desire for silence and interior prayer increased and heightened as a result of their generosity to him. He also speaks of the experience of his *starets'* spirit that seems to penetrate him as the wife reads from the book on the Our Father and enlightens him to instruct them in the mystical meaning of this most important of Christian prayers.

Most importantly, he tells them that the holy Fathers have written and taught that unceasing prayer of the heart is meant not merely for the select few who lock themselves away in monasteries, but for everyone. In his relationship to the master and his wife, the Pilgrim clearly takes on the role of a spiritual guide. By introducing them to the teachings of the holy Fathers in *The Philokalia* about unceasing prayer, he more than repays them for their kindness to him. They feed him, clothe him, and give him shelter; he provides them with that all-important lens with which they can open up the deep spiritual meaning of the Scriptures.

One important sign that the Pilgrim is functioning as a spiritual guide for these kindhearted people is the way he attentively listens to the wife tell of the family's background. By walking through the garden with her after the meal and allowing her to explain how her family got to their present state of happiness, the Pilgrim allows the woman to express the key events that have shaped her life, and to rejoice in the way God's hand has manifested itself through them. Her relationship to her mother is particularly important to the way she understands herself and her duty before God. That she and her husband have so meticulously carried out her spiritual instructions for the last ten years is a sign of their deep desire to grow in their relationship to God. The coming of the Pilgrim into their lives signals a call to growth. By introducing them to the mysteries of the interior prayer of the heart, he gives them the opportunity to integrate their charitable works with a rich inner life that only God can bestow.

Finally, the Pilgrim not only serves as a spiritual guide for both husband and wife but he also learns from them. This comes out most clearly when he is startled by the lack of interest the priest shows regarding reading at table or, so it seems, any kind of learning at all. The Pilgrim, at first, shudders at this seeming lack of respect for the wisdom of God's Word, but soon learns from the wife of the house that he should not judge the priest. By listening to her, he is reminded of the words of Nikitas Stethatos in *The Philokalia*: "He who has attained to true prayer and love has no sense of the differences between things. He does not distinguish the righteous man from the sinner, but loves them all equally and judges no man, as God causes his sun to shine and his rain to fall on the just and the unjust."[52] Just as the Pilgrim is humble enough to learn from those he is teaching, spiritual directors must likewise be open to learn about the spiritual life from those they direct. They should be ready to listen to the voice of God wherever it comes from.

The Pilgrim Encounters a Blind Beggar: Summary

It is when he is sitting at table with this pious family and their assorted group of guests that the Pilgrim notices a blind beggar, whose mouth is constantly opened and whose tongue keeps moving inside, as if it were trembling. The Pilgrim searches this man out after the siesta and asks him if, by any chance, he is praying the Jesus Prayer. The blind beggar affirms that this is so and adds that he cannot live without it. He tells the Pilgrim that he once belonged to a local guild and had earned his living as a tailor. He was once in a small village making clothing for a peasant family when he noticed three books lying by their icon case. Since no one in this family knew how to read, he picked up one of the books, opened it at random, and read words that he still remembers to this day: "Ceaseless prayer is to call upon the name of God always. Whether a man is conversing or sitting down or walking or making something or eating—whatever he may be doing—in all places and at all times, he ought to call upon God's name."[53] He tells the Pilgrim how he started praying to God in this way, but eventually stopped moving his lips when others started to notice him and jeer at him. He says that he has grown quite accustomed to praying like this and now finds it quite pleasant. He also says that he continued moving about, applying his trade until he became blind. He was on his way to an alms house in Tobolsk when he came upon the master and the mistress of this house, who urged him to stay with them until they could provide him with a cart to take him there.

Upon hearing the blind beggar's story, the Pilgrim opens *The Philokalia* to part four and reads a passage by Patriarch Callistus. This is the exact passage that the blind beggar had read so many years before. The Pilgrim continues reading and, when he gets to the part about praying with one's heart, is asked all sorts of questions about its possible meaning. It is then that the Pilgrim comes up with the idea of going to Tobolsk by foot with the man. In this way, he says he can read to him everything concerning the prayer of the heart, especially how to locate the place of the heart and how to enter into it. The blind man agrees to forgo the comforts of the cart and to walk with the Pilgrim, side by side, in order to learn more about the interior prayer of the heart.

The very next day, they take their leave of their hosts, and the Pilgrim begins reading from *The Philokalia* in the order he had been taught by his late *starets*, beginning with the book of Nicephorus the Solitary, Saint Gregory of Sinai, and so on. When he finishes reading all of this, the blind beggar begins asking him some difficult questions about how the mind can find the heart, how to bring the name of Jesus into it, and how to experience the delightful interior prayer of the heart. The Pilgrim then begins to instruct the beggar on his own, step by step, until the man is able to experience the power of this prayer for himself.

One interesting event occurs just prior to their arrival at Tobolsk. As they are walking through the forest, the blind beggar has a premonition of a burning church. The Pilgrim warns him not to place his trust in visions as signs of grace, because they can often be explained in a natural way, and can easily distract one from the way of unceasing prayer. When they finally arrive in the city, however, the two men find that the blind man's vision has actually come to pass. When questioned about this, the Pilgrim tells the beggar that he can interpret the situation as he wishes, but stands his ground about the caution one should place in such visions.

The Pilgrim leaves the blind beggar in Tobolsk. As he continues his journey, he reviews *The Philokalia* in order to verify all that he has told the man. In that process, he himself experiences even more intensely the delights of the interior prayer of the heart, so much so that he wishes that he might die as soon as possible so that he can pour out his heart in gratitude to God. This experience, however, soon becomes tempered by fear and anxiety, which in turn are countered by a determination to do God's will whatever that may be. This episode ends with the Pilgrim's recognition that even those whom he has recently introduced to the ways of unceasing prayer

had been directly prepared by God's hidden guidance long before
he met them.

Reflection

This is an important memory for the Pilgrim for a number of reasons. First, it is his first recollection of instructing someone in the
way of interior prayer who has already had some familiarity with
the Jesus Prayer. Elsewhere in his travels, he has met people who
led good lives, but who had doubts about their faith; at other times,
he encountered people who led pious lives full of charitable works,
but who were unfamiliar with the practice of unceasing prayer. This
is the first time he meets anyone who knows something about this
type of prayer and yet still has much more to learn about it. By
deciding to set out with the man on foot to Tobolsk, the Pilgrim
creates an atmosphere where he can lead the blind beggar more
deeply into the mysteries of interior prayer.

Second, the Pilgrim does so not only by reading passages of
The Philokalia (in the order suggested by his late *starets*) but also
through his own words and explanations. While these are ultimately
based in the teaching of the holy Fathers, they, nevertheless, bear
his own interpretative mark and represent a major step in his becoming a spiritual guide for others. The Pilgrim has incorporated
the teachings of *The Philokalia* so much within himself that, like
his *starets* before him, he feels free enough to put the book aside
and explain the mysteries of unceasing prayer on his own. This means
that he has internalized the teachings of the holy Fathers and is able
to speak about the practice of the interior prayer of the heart directly from his own experience.

Third, when doing so, the memory of his beloved *starets* is
never far from him. This comes across most clearly when the
Pilgrim warns the blind beggar of being cautious when it comes
to visions and premonitions about things to come, even though
what the blind man foresees actually comes to pass. Although
he cannot explain it, the Pilgrim sticks to his original caution-

ary advice, rather than get caught up in other such visionary forewarnings.

Fourth, once the Pilgrim leaves the blind beggar at Tobolsk and continues his journey, he takes great pains to go over *The Philokalia* to verify all that he has told the man about the prayer of the heart. This shows that the Pilgrim is concerned about the authenticity of what he has said. Even though he feels free enough from *The Philokalia* to let go of it and allow his instruction to be more spontaneous, he knows enough of his own weakness and limitations to go back to the source of his knowledge and to confirm all that he has said. Doing this both strengthens his own grasp of the material and gives him a deeper experience of the interior prayer of the heart itself.

Finally, the Pilgrim's experience of being a spiritual guide for the blind man provides him with an opportunity for further reflection on the significance of the interior prayer of the heart for his own life. This episode ends with the Pilgrim recounting how his own interior prayer of the heart is deepened as a result of his encounter with the blind beggar and of his conviction that God is at work in the lives of those who are guided spiritually, long before he ever meets them.

Each of these insights has much to say about spiritual direction. Like the Pilgrim, directors must be prepared to deal with people at various stages of their spiritual journey; they must journey with them, listen to them, and teach them. They must also share their own personal experience with their directees. When doing so, it is important that they themselves be in touch with the sources of spiritual knowledge that have been the most help to them in their lives; they must verify what they say to their directees and reflect on the significance of the process of direction for the directees and for their own lives. Most of all, it is essential that they recognize the gentle guiding hand of God in the lives of the people they deal with.

The Pilgrim's Stay in a Post Office: Summary

The Pilgrim tells his spiritual father that it is raining so hard one day that he needs to look for a place where he can dry off and spend the night. He eventually comes across an old drunk in a soldier's cloak standing outside a small dwelling. This gruff and belligerent man happens to be the local postmaster. After checking the Pilgrim's papers and making sure that they are all in order, he allows the Pilgrim entrance and offers him food and shelter from the storm.

Once inside, the Pilgrim is served something to eat by a young peasant woman, who also seems to have had a bit too much to drink. The postmaster and the servant woman quarrel during the entire meal and, eventually, end up fighting. When the postmaster finally goes to bed, the woman starts clearing the tables and the Pilgrim looks for a place where he can stretch out for the night. The woman points out a place for him and, just as he is about to fall asleep, a window shatters, the house starts shaking, and all sorts of commotion can be heard outside. The woman springs back in terror and goes crashing to the floor. The Pilgrim shoots out of his bed half conscious, thinking that the ground under him has split open.

As it turns out, a royal courier has been making his way to the post office for a change of horses and his coach driver miscalculates the turn into the gates. As a result, the carriage pole knocks out the window and the wagon turns over in a ditch in front of the house. Even though he is badly injured, the royal courier has no time to waste and is on his way after bathing his wound in water and wine and gulping down a quick glass of wine. The now unconscious peasant woman is dragged over to a corner of the room and is covered with blanket. The postmaster, who by this time has awakened from his slumber, has another drink and soon goes back to bed.

The Pilgrim departs the next morning and probably would have forgotten the entire incident had it not been for the fact that some six years later he is in a women's monastery, enjoying the hospitality of their table, when he asks the humble woman serving him how long she has been in the monastery. As it turns out, she is the very woman who had the terrifying experience in the post office some six years earlier. She tells the Pilgrim that she went mad from fear and, for an entire year, her family did not know what to do with her. They eventually took her from shrine to shrine, and it was not until they brought her to this monastery that she was healed. Upon hearing this, the Pilgrim rejoices and glorifies God who so wisely orders all things for the good.

Reflection
From one perspective, this episode tells us very little about the interior prayer of the heart or of the practice of spiritual guidance. The Pilgrim teaches the postmaster and the young peasant woman nothing about these important matters of the spiritual life. From another perspective, however, it has everything in the world to do with them, since it is a story about conversion.

To understand the significance of this passage, it is important to see it in relationship to the Pilgrim's words about God's providence at the end of his journey with the blind beggar. God's hidden guidance works in the hearts of people long before the Pilgrim meets them. To carry this statement one step further, God's hidden guidance is at work in people's lives even when the Pilgrim has very little to do with them. The episode at the post office is one such instance. As far as the Pilgrim can tell, the drunken postmaster and this young peasant woman have little knowledge of prayer and little interest in the things of the spirit. Their inordinate love of wine and their constant bickering are just external symptoms of their underlying spiritual unrest. God uses the carriage incident, by just about every other count a most unfortunate affair, as an instrument of the young woman's conversion. The Pilgrim rejoices in seeing God's hand at work, even in the most difficult of circumstances.

In this incident, the Pilgrim plays only a peripheral role in the conversion of the young woman. He is a mere accessory, someone who merely observes what is taking place but who has no real input in the change of heart that ultimately comes about. When he real-

izes that the nun pouring him tea is the same person who lost her
wits in the post office so long ago, he realizes how God is the sole
person responsible for the great change that has taken place. From
this perspective, the Pilgrim realizes that all things—the prayer of
the heart, spiritual guidance, even conversion—ultimately come
from the hand of the Lord. All he or anyone else can do is just
cooperate with the movement of God's grace and continually hope
for the best.

In a similar vein, spiritual directors must recognize that, in the
vast scheme of things, it is ultimately God who moves the hearts of
the people they deal with. Directors must be careful not to attribute
more to their efforts than is called for. They must be willing to step
back and give God the credit for what he is accomplishing in the
lives of their directees.

The Pilgrim Recounts Two Brief Village
Experiences: Summary

The Pilgrim goes on to tell his spiritual director that so many
unusual things happened to him in his journeys that he would,
at this point, need at least three days to cover them all. He ends
his account of his recollections on the road with two brief stories.

The first has to do with his visit to a young but frail-looking
priest in a small village. The Pilgrim attends this priest's liturgy and
is impressed with the man's devotion in reciting the words. The
priest invites the Pilgrim to his home and tells him that prayer without interior appreciation and feeling is useless. In his mind: "[t]o
attain spiritual enlightenment and become a man of recollected
interior life, you should take some one text of holy Scripture
and for as long a period as possible, concentrate on that alone
all your power of attention and meditation; then the light of understanding will be revealed to you."[54] The Pilgrim says that he
rejoices in this humble shepherd of the flock of Christ and gives
thanks to God all the more when he discovers in the man's house-

hold an elderly woman who has prayed the Jesus Prayer ever since her youth.

The second incident goes back to when the Pilgrim passes through the Kazan province and has to spend the night in a Tartar village. There he befriends a Russian coachman and hears his story of how his wife abandoned him when he got sick and elderly, and how he drew comfort only from reciting the Jesus Prayer. The Pilgrim also hears the man tell of how he raised his godson on the prayer and even went so far as to hold a cane close by to prod him into reciting it. Eventually, the man's godson got so used to reciting the prayer that he could not live without it. Upon his death, he tasted the fruits of prayer to a greater degree than his godfather did in his old age.

Reflection

These incidents affirm the wide range of people whose lives can be affected by the Jesus Prayer. They point out that the prayer is for all of us, regardless of age, sex, education, or station in life. The priest, the elderly woman, and the coachman and his godson start out reciting the prayer with different intentions. One seeks to pray the liturgy with fervor and devotion; another wishes to invoke the protection of God in her travels; another seeks comfort in the midst of sickness and old age; still another is literally forced into it. Regardless of their intentions, all of them eventually come to experience a deep sense of inner peace from the prayer. What is more, they all recognize its importance for their lives and take great pains to practice it with fervor and devotion. In all of this, the Pilgrim rejoices in how God works in the lives of these people. When listening to their stories, he recognizes that, in one way or another, God makes his hand manifest in everyone's life, not just in his own. Listening to these people's stories puts his own story in perspective and makes him all the more grateful for what God has done for him.

THE PILGRIM DEPARTS FOR JERUSALEM

Summary and Reflection

After finishing his stories, the Pilgrim apologizes to his spiritual father for talking so long. He refers to the holy Fathers who "call even spiritual talk mere babble if it lasts too long."[55] He tells his spiritual father that it is now time for him to take his leave to find his fellow traveler to Jerusalem. He asks his spiritual father to pray for him, a miserable sinner, and especially to ask that God grant him a good journey. His spiritual father bids him well and asks God's abundant blessings to go with him on his journey.

This concluding section ends with the Pilgrim setting out on his long journey to Jerusalem. Since it has only barely gotten underway, the particulars of that journey are left for us to imagine. At this point, no one knows if the Pilgrim will ever make it there. The road lies before him and all he really has to rely on is the mercy and protection of God. Without that, there is no hope at all of his ever reaching his final destination.

With his thoughts clearly focused on the journey ahead of him, the author is now ready to end his narrative. He has looked back to his past, not for the sake of looking back, but in order to gain a better perspective on where he has come from and where he is going. At this point, he leaves both his spiritual father *and* his readers behind. Since his journey is still taking shape, it cannot yet be looked back on and reflected upon, and certainly not yet written down. What the future holds for him—for us—must be left in the hands of Providence and will be known only as it unfolds.

CONCLUSION

As we close the book, our minds certainly set to wondering about the Pilgrim, but more so about our own journey toward Jerusalem and the companions with whom we are traveling. What lies ahead for us? What difficulties will we encounter? What trials will we endure? What displays of kindness will we receive from the hands of total strangers and how will we respond?

The Pilgrim's journey to Jerusalem is not laid out for us because, by this time, our journey and the Pilgrim's journey have become one. The story of this simple peasant of the most humble origins has, by the end of the journey, stamped itself on our consciousness and has become a metaphor of the journey that each of us, whatever our origins, must ultimately take. By this time, we have walked with the anonymous author through four distinct narratives that have taught us much about the mysteries of the interior prayer of the heart and the nature of a sound relationship of spiritual guidance. It is the author's hope that what he has written of his travels will help us make our own way to Jerusalem. That this journey is not ended is symptomatic of our world. Before us lies the open road. Just what it holds in the days, months, years ahead, no one knows for certain. Such is the nature of the Pilgrim's way. Such is the journey we all must make when we seek to follow in the footsteps of the Lord Jesus and to have unceasing recourse in our hearts to the power and glory of his name.

REFLECTION QUESTIONS

1. The Pilgrim postpones his plans because he agrees to help an elderly deaf man make his way toward Jerusalem. Are you willing to go out of your way in order to help another person? Are you willing to do so even if it means changing your plans for an extended period of time? If so, for how long? a day? a week? a month? a year? Are you able to accept such help from another when you are in a similar situation? For how long? Do you use certain criteria to decide if and when you are going to help someone? Are these criteria valid? Do they reflect the values of the gospel?

2. Because of his change in plans, the Pilgrim has another opportunity to visit his spiritual father and, this time, to tell him about some of the educational experiences he has had during his life of wandering. If asked, which events in *your* life would you highlight as being the most educational? Have you ever shared these experiences with another? If so, with whom? If not, why not? Would you feel comfortable sharing them with your spiritual director? Can you think of any instances in which you contributed to another's spiritual education? Have you ever shared these experiences with another person? Are you willing to take the risk?

3. The Pilgrim's late *starets* appears to him in a dream and tells him that he will encounter on his journeys theft from the left-hand side (sinful imaginings) and theft from the right-hand side (edifying thoughts) that will attempt to lure him away from prayer. How do you deal with temptation? Have you ever felt lured away from prayer? Are you hounded more by temptations of "left-handed" or "right-handed" theft? What do you do when you weaken and fall? How do you go about asking for God's forgiveness? Are you able to accept it? How do you go about asking the forgiveness from others? Do you forgive others easily or do you hold a grudge against them and always look for ways to get back at them?

4. "For I was hungry and you gave me food, I was thirsty and you gave me drink. I was a stranger and you welcomed me" (Mt 25:35). For much of this narrative, the Pilgrim receives the hospitality of a devout Christian family. Have you ever enjoyed the hospitality of near-total strangers? What was the experience like? How did you feel? How did their hospitality enrich you? What lessons did they impart to you? Did you reciprocate in any way? How does the Pilgrim reciprocate? How would Jesus reciprocate?

5. Among his other educational experiences, the Pilgrim tells of the time he instructed a blind beggar in the subtleties of the Jesus

Prayer. What would you say if you found yourself in such a situation? How would you begin? What texts would you use? What exercises would you suggest? How would you present the Jesus Prayer as a way of constant prayer? What images would you employ? What benefits would you highlight? What creative approaches might you take? Do you think you would learn from such an experience?

6. As in the case of the pious Christian family and the blind beggar, the Pilgrim is humble enough to learn from those he is teaching. Can the same be said for you? Are you open to the truth wherever it comes from, or do you use your knowledge as a way of highlighting your own self-importance? Are you able to admit your mistakes or do you try to cover them up in order to preserve your respectability? Do you try to learn from the wisdom of others or do you believe that others can tell you nothing that you do not already know?

7. In this narrative, the Pilgrim takes great pains to verify his experiences against what he has read in *The Philokalia*. How do you make sure that your own spiritual experiences are truly rooted in the Christian tradition? What criteria do you use? Which books do you refer to? What people do you consult? In what ways does spiritual direction enter into this process of judgment? If you are a spiritual director, do you enable your directees to arrive at such judgments? If so, how?

8. In this narrative, the Pilgrim demonstrates, by both his words and actions, that he is becoming more and more a self-directed individual. That is to say that he has incorporated the values of the gospel, *The Philokalia*, and his *starets* into his life and is able to act accordingly. Do you consider yourself a self-directed individual? If so, which teachings, books, and people have you incorporated into your spiritual outlook on life? If not, what can you do to become such a person?

9. In this narrative, the Pilgrim demonstrates a deep sense of God's providential care. Do you believe that God plays an active role in your life? in the lives of others? in the history of the world? If so, how and to what extent? In the events of your day, do you recognize a personal invitation on God's part for you to participate in the spreading of the gospel and the gradual transformation of the world? How do these gospel beliefs manifest themselves in the concrete circumstances of your life? How do they show themselves in your relationships with the people you encounter on a day-to-day basis?

10. At the end of the narrative, the Pilgrim must take leave of his spiritual father and begin his journey to Jerusalem. This separation points symbolically to his coming of age as a mature individual who is led by the Spirit, and to his willingness to face the dangers and vicissitudes of the journey ahead. How do you deal with separation from those you care about? Do you experience it as a kind of death? Do you miss them? Do you sense their presence with you even though you are separated by long distances? Do you have a spiritual father or mother? Do you feel as though you are ready to leave that person and to set out on your journey to Jerusalem? Are you ready to leave behind some of the structures you hold dear and set out on your own with the Spirit in your heart—with the Lord on your one side and with someone who needs your help on the other?

EXERCISES

1. Write a letter to Jesus asking him to help you welcome the unexpected in your life. Ask him to help you live your life in such a way that you will be able to understand the needs of others and that you will be able and willing to adapt your plans in order to help them. Make the letter as long as you want it to be: a few words, a couple of paragraphs, a number of pages. You might want to dictate it into a tape recorder. When you finish, read it over (or play it back). Hold

on to it. Keep it close to your bed so that you can refer to it before you go to sleep and/or when you awake.

2. Imagine that Jesus is going to visit your neighborhood and that you have been asked to host an evening reception of about twenty-five people to welcome him. Who would you invite? What would you serve? What would you do to offer hospitality to Jesus and your guests and to make them all feel at home? What precautions would you take? After reflecting on this situation for a few minutes, read the words of Matthew 25:45 and ask yourself why this reception should be any different from any other you have hosted.

3. Make up your own version of the Jesus Prayer. Do so by finding a verse or phrase from the Gospels that means a great deal to you or that you find particularly impelling (for example, "I assure you, unless you change and become like little children, you shall not enter the kingdom of God," Mt 18:3). Repeat this saying often. Use your own words if you think it would help (for example, "Help me, Lord, to become like a little child"). Recite this prayer as often as you can throughout the day. As you do so, ask the Lord to help you one day to pray this prayer without ceasing.

4. Make a list of all the people in your life whom you feel you have influenced for the better. Be sure to list your friends and family, those you have ministered to (perhaps in the context of spiritual direction), and those you have helped only in passing. Next to each name write how you influenced that person and how that person, in turn, influenced you. If this project seems overwhelming, limit your efforts to the past month, year, or as you see fit. When you finish, close your eyes and imagine where these people would be if you had never been born. Try to imagine what the world would be like if you had never existed and there was no one to take your place in the situations you have just described. Then open your eyes and, reciting the Jesus Prayer, thank the Lord for the gift of life and the

many opportunities you have been given to share with others the gospel of life.

5. Think of life as a motion picture and you are one of the characters in it. Imagine yourself as the leading actor or actress. What does it feel like to be the center of attention and to have such a leading role in the outcome of the plot? Are you comfortable with being at the center of things? Can you stand the pressure? Would you rather be elsewhere? Next imagine yourself as a supporting actor or actress with less of a decisive role in the film. What does it feel like to be in this role? Are you satisfied in it? Are you unhappy in that role? Would you rather have the leading part? Now imagine yourself as a secondary character, someone on the periphery of events who has little influence on the outcome of events. What does it feel like to be just another face in the crowd? Do you enjoy your anonymity? Are you threatened by it? When you have finished imagining these various situations, think of Jesus as the director who asks you, at various times, to play any one of these and other roles in the vast action-packed cinema of life. End by asking him for help in what he is currently asking you to do, realizing that tomorrow you may be called on to play a very different role.

Conclusion

A t the end of our treatment of spiritual guidance in *The Way of a Pilgrim*, a concise summary of our findings is in order. Our aim here is not only to recapitulate, as briefly and clearly as possible, the spiritual teaching presented in the book but also to highlight the relevance it has for the developing ministry of spiritual direction in the Church.

SUMMARY

1. To begin with, "remembering" plays an important role in our coming to understand the movement of God's hand in our life. The book contains the Pilgrim's recollection of how he comes to a knowledge of the meaning of unceasing prayer in his early life, as well as his reflections on his childhood and early life. It is in remembering that an event is fully experienced; without it, there is not enough distance in our life to perceive where we have come from and where we may be being led.

2. For this reason, spiritual directors should encourage their directees to share their story of how they have experienced God in their lives. This means creating an atmosphere of trust so that directees will feel free enough to share even painful and embarrassing moments. It also means being willing to listen to directees in an active, non-threatening way, so that they are able to reflect back the events they have related. Like the Pilgrim's spiritual father, spiritual directors

should be able to help their directees to share and interpret the story of their ongoing relationship with God.

3. The book places a great emphasis on the invocation of Jesus' name, whether with the lips, in the mind, or in the heart. As such, it presents an understanding of prayer that is possible for all people, regardless of age, sex, occupation, or state in life. Prayer is nothing more than talking to God. The more we talk to God the closer we draw to God. As we draw closer to God—like the Pilgrim—the quality of our prayer deepens and reverberates throughout every dimension of human existence.

4. Spiritual directors should thus help their directees take a look at the way they pray. What role, if any, does Jesus play? Does their prayer address every anthropological level of human existence? Do they make prayer out to be more complicated than it really is? Do they take the risk of having a plain, simple heart-to-heart talk with God? These are just some of the questions that spiritual directors should help their directees address. By doing so, directors enable their directees to sift through the various experiences of prayer they have in their lives and find the right balance of form or forms that will best work for them.

5. The book places great hope in the Jesus Prayer as a way of praying to God without ceasing (see 1 Thess 5:17). It does not present this prayer as a magical incantation that automatically draws a person closer to God, but as an expression of a relationship that already exists and is forever deepening. As such, it offers even a person like the Pilgrim a simple way of sharing with God the innermost desires of one's heart and the space within oneself to listen attentively to the Lord's own heartfelt response.

6. Directors should thus be ready to offer the Jesus Prayer to their directees as a viable option for their spiritual lives. In doing so, they

should be able to explain its various nuances and be capable of dealing with any difficulties that might arise. As the *starets* does with the Pilgrim, directors should be able to meet their directees where they are and lead them step-by-step along the way of continuous prayer and communion with the Spirit of God. At the same time, they must be careful not to force this particular prayer form on their directees or present it in such a way that it is the only one with any validity.

7. The book places a great deal of emphasis on the role of sacred Scripture in spiritual formation. It does so especially by promoting a slow, reflective reading of it and by encouraging us to allow the words to sink in and settle in our soul. Only in this way will the Word of God truly be able to take root in our heart. Only in this way will we be able to respond to that Word in the concrete circumstances of life.

8. Directors should thus be able to help their directees interpret their lives in the light of sacred Scripture. They should be so immersed in the Word of God themselves that, when directees share their stories, they will be able to detect specific patterns that resonate between the Word of God and the stories. When doing so, they should be discerning enough to know when to challenge and when to console. They should also be prepared to offer their directees specific Scripture texts that may be helpful for them to reflect upon as they continue their spiritual journey.

9. The book also places great value on *The Philokalia* as an interpretive guide to the Scriptures. It considers it a powerful lens that enables us to look upon the dazzling light of God's revelation. As such, it should be read meditatively and reflected upon whenever we get the chance. Like the Pilgrim who possesses his own copy of it and who carries it with him wherever he goes, we are encouraged to immerse ourselves in this holy collection of sayings and treatises

on prayer. In doing so, our reading of *The Way* will become even more meaningful and alive.

10. Spiritual directors should thus make a point of being well versed in the sayings of *The Philokalia* and of being ready to lead their directees through its highly concentrated and enigmatic teachings. Since *The Way* presents the spiritual teaching of *The Philokalia* in an uncompromising yet accessible way, directors would do well to offer it as an initial point of departure for unlocking the secrets of the much larger work. At all times, directors should remember that neither the *starets* nor the Pilgrim ever force these teachings on anyone, but offer them freely to those interested in deepening their relationship with the Lord.

11. The book has a positive outlook toward dreams as a vehicle through which we can come to learn the will of God. The *starets* appears to the Pilgrim a number of times in his dreams and leads him to particular passages of *The Philokalia* that are more suited to the present stage of his spiritual journey. The *starets* also warns the Pilgrim of certain dangers that lay ahead of him and how he should react once he comes up against them. In a similar way, directors should encourage their directees to pay attention to their dreams and to adopt methods of interpretation that will help them come to a deeper understanding of their spiritual journey.

12. The book places a great deal of emphasis on finding God in the concrete circumstances of life. It affirms over and over again that God speaks to us through the events of the day. By immersing himself in the Bible, the teachings of *The Philokalia*, and the depths of unceasing prayer, the Pilgrim finds that he is better able to read and interpret what happens to him in the light of God's plan for him. This enables him to find meaning in the various situations that come his way and to deal with them in a manner that becomes a Christian.

13. Directors should likewise help their directees, using whatever means are available, to look for God in the concrete circumstances of their lives. In this way, directors will gradually enable their directees to come to a deeper understanding of the ramifications of the Incarnation for their lives (that is, Jesus as Emmanuel, "God-with-us"). By motivating their directees to enter into the present moment and to embrace the concrete situation in which they find themselves, directors help their directees acknowledge their current responsibilities in life and set them in the right path for discerning what God is calling them to do.

14. The book emphasizes the difficulty the Pilgrim has in finding a qualified director (that is, someone who can explain to him the meaning of unceasing prayer). As such, it brings to the fore the common difficulty many people have today in finding someone who understands the ways of the Spirit and who is capable of accompanying them on their spiritual journey. Just as the *starets* leads the Pilgrim step-by-step through the various nuances of the Jesus Prayer, so too must directors be able and willing to accompany their directees on every step of the way in their walk with the Lord.

15. The book inspires reflection on the nature of the bond between director and directee. The *starets* and the Pilgrim are involved in a living spiritual relationship that goes beyond the bounds of "professional" courtesy—a relationship that is entirely focused on the deepest desire of the *hesychast* tradition, that is, to pray without ceasing. In a similar vein, directors need to examine the nature and strength of the bonds they share with their directees. Are the bonds strong or weak? Do director and directee enjoy a living spiritual relationship that has knitted their spirits together? Are the limits to the relationship clear and well thought out?

16. The book places a high value on honesty in the spiritual-direction relationship. The Pilgrim holds nothing back from his *starets* re-

garding his difficulties in prayer (for example, distractions, boredom, loss of fervor). As a result, the *starets* has an accurate picture of the Pilgrim's inner life and is better able to prescribe appropriate remedies from *The Philokalia*. This freedom to share everything is a characteristic of the depth of relationship shared by the Pilgrim and his *starets*. Directors and directees should likewise regularly ask themselves if they are truly being honest with each other, if the process of direction is truly helpful (or just *pro forma*), if they are avoiding certain subjects out of fear (or convenience).

17. The book emphasizes the humility of the director before the tradition. The *starets* recognizes his own limitations and introduces the Pilgrim to the riches of *The Philokalia*. As a result, the *starets* and the Pilgrim establish a bond that extends beyond the *starets'* death and that continues to support the Pilgrim in his subsequent journey through life. This bond is so strong that it carries the Pilgrim through some of his most difficult times, when he does not know what to do or where to turn. In a similar vein, directors should be humble enough to recognize what they do not know, admit their mistakes, and be willing to learn from their directees.

18. The book relates the story of someone who is becoming more and more self-directive in his spiritual journey. At the outset of his search for the meaning of unceasing prayer, the Pilgrim is dependent on spiritual guides and other external helps, especially that of the *starets* and *The Philokalia*. As time goes on, however, he internalizes these important structures and is increasingly able to rely on his own powers of judgment to discern the Lord's will in his life. That is not to say that he is entirely independent of them or that he never again needs to have recourse to them. It means only that he has grown mature enough in his relationship with the Lord to determine for himself what needs to be done in the circumstances of his daily life.

19. In a similar vein, directors should look upon the relationship of spiritual direction as one that encourages directees to internalize those structures upon which they rely for help. Directors should encourage their directees to become less and less dependent on the outward display of the direction process itself and thus become more self-directive in the decisions they make about their lives. The purpose of spiritual direction is not to perpetuate the external trappings of the director/directee relationship for their own sake. Instead, it should allow the relationship to deepen and be transformed in such a way that the directee becomes less and less dependent on it for spiritual well-being.

20. Finally, the book looks to the Holy Spirit as the director of the spiritual life *par excellence*. As the Pilgrim's story progresses, it becomes increasingly clear that he is being led not by his own whims and desires but by the desires of the Spirit. That is to say that his spiritual journey has brought him so close to God that he now thinks, speaks, and acts in harmony with the Spirit of God, who communes with him in the depths of his soul. All other helps for spiritual guidance are seen as instruments of the Spirit. They are helpful only because the Spirit uses them as a means of leading the Pilgrim to a deeper knowledge of God in the concrete circumstances of his life.

CONCLUSION

The above summary in no way exhausts the wealth of insights on the theme of spiritual guidance that has been uncovered in *The Way of a Pilgrim*. It does provide the main currents of thought that have surfaced in this study, and qualifies as a point of departure for further reflection on the topic. What is more, it brings to the fore the many close connections that can be drawn between the Pilgrim's intense desire to learn the meaning of unceasing prayer and the ministry of spiritual direction. Hopefully, these connections will encourage both directors and directees to use the book as a point of reference for their ongoing conversations about God, life, and the nature of prayer.

Recall that the fourfold method of summary, reflection, query, and activity, used throughout this work, is open-ended and, as such, invites us to keep the process going long after the final activity has been completed. This fourfold method asks us to go back over the various incidents found in the four narratives of *The Way* and to reflect on their meaning for our own lives. It also encourages us to ask pertinent questions about life in light of these reflections and to determine some concrete activities that will bring us further along the way of conversion.

What is offered in these pages is nothing more than one person's fragile (and very limited) attempt to relate one of the classics of Orthodox spirituality to the contemporary ministry of spiritual direction. The reading, while by no means complete, has brought to the fore a number of valid points of comparison that should be of help to directors and directees in their attempt to draw closer to God. Bearing these limitations in mind, we are encouraged to continue the process of discovery and to delve even further into the mysteries of unceasing prayer.

> *"Lord Jesus Christ, have mercy on me."*
> THE JESUS PRAYER

Suggested Readings

Amlaw, Mary. *From Praying Never to Praying Always*. New York: Pueblo Publishing Co., 1985.

Brainchaninov, I. *On the Prayer of Jesus*. London: Watkins, 1952.

Breck, J. "Prayer of the Heart: Sacrament of the Presence of God." *Saint Vladimir's Theological Quarterly* 39 (1995): 25–45.

Corbishley, Thomas. *The Prayer of Jesus*. Garden City, NY: Doubleday, 1977.

Corneanu, N. "The Jesus Prayer and Deification." *Saint Vladimir's Theological Quarterly* 39 (1995): 3–24.

De Melo, Carlo. "Union with God through the Jesus Prayer." *Spiritual Life* 38 (1992): 91–93.

Every, G. "The Study of Eastern Orthodoxy: Hesychasm." *Religion* 9 (1979): 73–91.

Fedotov, G. P. *The Russian Religious Mind*. 2 vols. Cambridge, MA: Harvard University Press, 1946–66.

Giardini, Fabio. "Unceasing Prayer." *Angelicum* 72 (1995): 281–312.

Goettmann, Alphonse, and Rachel Goettmann. *Prayer of Jesus— Prayer of the Heart*. Translated by Th. and R. Nottingham. New York/Mahwah, NJ: Paulist Press, 1991.

Healy, Kathleen. *Entering the Cave of the Heart. Eastern Ways of Prayer for Western Christians*. New York/Mahwah, NJ: Paulist Press, 1986.

Kallistos of Diokleia. "Praying with the Body: The *Hesychast* Method and Non-Christian Parallels." *Sobornost* 14 (1992): 5–22.

Maloney, George A. *Prayer of the Heart*. Notre Dame, IN: Ave Maria Press, 1981.

Meany, J. O. and M. Casey. "Psychology and 'The Prayer of the Heart.'" *Review for Religious* 29 (1970): 818–26.

Ware, Kallistos. "The Origins of the Jesus Prayer: Diadochus, Gaza, Sinai." Chap. in *The Study of Spirituality*, eds. Cheslyn Jones, Geoffrey Wainwright, and Edward Yarnold. London: SPCK, 1986; second impression, 1992.

Notes

1. The text used in this study comes from *The Way of a Pilgrim*, translated by R. M. French. Milwaukee, WI: Morehouse Publishing Company, 1931.
2. *The Philokalia: The Complete Text*, trans. and eds., G.E.H. Palmer, Philip Sherrard and Kallistos Ware, 5 vols. (London/ Boston: Faber and Faber, 1979–95). According to Ronald J. Zawilla, "The four essential elements that distinguish Hesychasm are devotion to the name of Jesus, a keen sense of sorrow for sin, the discipline of frequent repetition, and a nondiscursive, imageless prayer leading to inner silence." See Downey, Michael, ed. *The New Dictionary of Catholic Spirituality* (Collegeville, MN: Michael Glazier/Liturgical Press, 1993), s.v. "Hesychasm."
3. *The Pilgrim Continues His Way* appeared in 1911 and was probably not written by the author of *The Way of a Pilgrim* (c. 1853–61). It takes up the story of the wandering *strannik* and employs the dialogue form rather than first person narration to go into many of the subtleties of the Jesus Prayer and the *hesychast* tradition. The two works first appeared together in 1930.
4. *Starets*, pl. *startsi*. A monk distinguished by his great piety, long experience of the spiritual life, and gift for guiding other souls. Lay folk frequently resort to *startsi* for spiritual counsel and, in a monastery, a new member of the community is attached to a *starets* who trains and teaches him.
5. *Philokalia* (in Russian: *Dobrotolyubie*). "The Love of Spiritual

Beauty." The title of the great collection of mystical and ascetic writings by Fathers of the Eastern Church, over a period of eleven centuries.

6. *The Way*, 1.
7. *The Way*, 1.
8. *The Way*, 3.
9. *The Way*, 4.
10. *The Way*, 4.
11. *The Way*, 7.
12. *The Way*, 8.
13. *The Way*, 9.
14. *The Way*, 10.
15. *The Way*, 10.
16. *The Way*, 10.
17. *The Way*, 10.
18. *The Way*, 11.
19. *The Way*, 11.
20. *The Way*, 20.
21. *Dyachok.* A minister whose chief liturgical function is to chant psalms and the Epistle in the Russian Church.
22. *Mir.* The assembly of all the peasant householders in a village. It was a very ancient institution, in which the peasants only had a voice, even the great landowners being excluded. The *mir* enjoyed a certain measure of self-government and elected representatives to the larger peasant assembly of the *volost,* which included several *mirs.* The *starosta* was the elected headman of the *mir.*
23. *Zavalina.* A bank of earth against the front wall of the house, flat-topped, and used as a seat.
24. *Priests.* The word is *ksendz,* which means a Polish priest of the Roman Catholic Church. The steward, being a Pole, was a Roman Catholic.
25. *The Way*, 22.
26. *The Way*, 23.

27. *The Way*, 34.
28. *The Way*, 42–43.
29. *The Way*, 46.
30. *The Way*, 46.
31. *The Way*, 49–50.
32. *The Way*, 51. See Ps 104:24.
33. *The Way*, 60.
34. *The Way*, 65.
35. *The Way*, 65.
36. *The Way*, 66.
37. This person is not the *starets* of the first two narratives, but a later spiritual guide.
38. *The Way*, 82.
39. *The Way*, 83.
40. *Skhimnik* (feminine, *skhimnitsa*). A monk (nun) of the highest grade. The distinction between simple and solemn vows, which has arisen in the West, has never found a place in Orthodox monasticism. In the latter, religious are of three grades, distinguished by their habits, and the highest grade is pledged to a stricter degree of asceticism and a greater amount of time spent in prayer. The Russian *skhimnik* is the Greek *megalo-schemos*.
41. *Icon.* The icon or sacred picture occupies a prominent position in Orthodox life. In Russia, icons are found not only in churches but in public buildings of all sorts, as well as in private houses. In the devout Russian's room, the icon will hang or rest on a shelf diagonally across a corner opposite the door, and a reverence will be made to it by a person entering or leaving the room.
42. *Onoochi.* Long strips of material, generally coarse linen, which the Russian peasant wraps round his feet and legs instead of wearing stockings.
43. *Bashmaki.* A kind of shoe.
44. *Altar.* In Orthodox churches, altar is the name of that part of the

building which is known in the West as the "sanctuary." What Westerners call the *altar* is, in the East, the *throne* or *holy table*. In Orthodox phraseology, the *throne* stands in the *altar*.

45. *Batyushka.* "Little Father," a familiar and affectionate form of address, applied usually to priests.
46. *Dark water.* The popular name for glaucoma.
47. The Tartars, of course, being Moslems.
48. *Samovar.* A sort of urn heated with charcoal to supply hot water for tea.
49. *The Way*, 86.
50. See *The Way*, 89.
51. *The Way*, 113.
52. *The Way*, 113–14.
53. *The Way*, 116.
54. *The Way*, 130–31.
55. *The Way*, 138.